Oo-pples and Boo-noo-noos

Songs and Activities for Phonemic Awareness, Second Edition

Hallie Kay Yopp • Ruth Helen Yopp

Harcourt

Orlando   Boston   Dallas   Chicago   San Diego

Visit *The Learning Site!*

www.harcourtschool.com

ISBN 0-15-325787-3

6 7 8 9 10 170 10 09 08 07 06 05 04 03

A Note About the Authors

Dr. Hallie Kay Yopp is a professor in the Department of Elementary, Bilingual, and Reading Education at California State University in Fullerton, where she teaches courses in reading and language arts and coordinates the graduate program. Known mostly for her work in phonemic awareness, she also writes and speaks about a wide variety of literacy topics to audiences across the nation. She has co-authored several books and serves on editorial advisory boards for reading journals. In addition, Hallie is on the author team for Harcourt where she has contributed to the reading, language arts, and social studies programs. Hallie taught elementary school for many years, including eight years in a bilingual setting, and continues to spend time in elementary classrooms. She and Ruth Yopp were the year 2000 inductees into the California Reading Hall of Fame.

Dr. Ruth Yopp, Hallie's identical twin sister, is also a professor of education at California State University, Fullerton. Her areas of interest include comprehension and vocabulary instruction, early literacy development, and content area reading. She has conducted many workshops on reading development from early literacy to fluent reading across the curriculum and is the author of numerous publications. Currently, she co-chairs the Department of Elementary, Bilingual, and Reading Education at the university and directs two teacher development projects and a teacher recruitment project. A former elementary school teacher, she also volunteers on a regular basis in her sons' elementary school classrooms.

Contents ♪♪♪

Page

Page

Creating a Phonemically Rich Classroom

These are exciting times for reading instruction! We have learned much from recent research, including studies of phonemic awareness, the understanding that words consist of a sequence of sounds (phonemes). Phonemically aware children are able to think about the sounds of words apart from their meanings. They can shift their attention from *fish* as an animal that swims in oceans to *fish* as a word that consists of three sounds: /f/-/i/-/sh/.

We have discovered in recent times that phonemic awareness is related to success in learning to read. In fact:

- Phonemic awareness is one of the most potent predictors of success in learning to read (Stanovich, 1994).
- Children who lack phonemic awareness are likely to be among our poorest readers (Blachman, 2000).

- Phonemic awareness is necessary but not sufficient for reading acquisition (Smith, Simmons, & Kameenui, 1998).

This is so because our written system records, for the most part, the smallest sounds of speech. Therefore, in order for the logic of the written system to be apparent, children must notice those small sounds in speech.

Included in this book are activities, chants, rhymes, poems, songs, and a list of recommended books that play with language in such a way as to draw children's attention to sounds. We hope you will teach them to your students and then find many occasions to revisit them. Recite a poem as you walk to the cafeteria, sing a song as you wait for snacks, read the books listed here over and over again. Comment on the language play. Encourage further language play.

By flooding your classroom with opportunities to experiment with and explore the sounds of language, you will be providing a phonemically rich environment and supporting your young students' literacy development.

Rhymes and Chants

There is a wonderful oral tradition in which rhymes and chants are passed from generation to generation and from one child to another. If you listen to children, you will hear them spontaneously repeating the rhythmic language they learn from others. Teachers can support children's emerging sensitivity to the sound structure of their language by capitalizing on their interest in rhymes and chants.

We share a variety of counting-out rhymes, jump-rope rhymes, nursery rhymes, and echo chants in this section. Many of them contain rhyming words. Others are alliterative or make use of phoneme additions or substitutions. Thus, they are well suited for drawing children's attention to sounds. You can share chants and rhymes throughout the day, and encourage children to repeat them, to change them, and to talk about them. These activities lay the groundwork for more advanced insights into the phonemic basis of speech.

Counting-Out Rhymes

Counting-out rhymes typically include rhyming words, nonsense words, and interesting sound patterns.

Eggs and ham,
Out you scram!

Inky, pinky, penny winky
Out goes she (or he).

Fireman, fireman, number eight.
Hit his head against the gate.
The gate flew in, the gate flew out.
That's the way he put the fire out.
O-U-T spells out, and out you go.

One potato, two potato,
Three potato, four,
Five potato, six potato,
Seven potato, more.

Sky blue, sky blue.
Who's it? Not you!

O-U-T spells out goes he,
Right in the middle of
    the deep, blue sea!

Two, four, six, eight,
Mary at the garden gate.
Eating cherries off a plate.
Two, four, six, eight.

Oh, dear me,
Momma caught a flea.
Flea died, Momma cried,
One, two, three.

Acka backa soda cracker,
Acka backa boo,
Acka backa soda cracker,
Out goes you!

Ickle, ockle, bottle,
Ickle, ockle, out.
If you come to my house,
I will send you out.
O-U-T spells out,
And out you go for saying so.

My mother, your mother
Live across the way,
Every night they put out the light,
And this is what they say:
Hinky, dinky,
Soda crackers,
Hinky, dinky, boo,
Hinky, dinky,
Soda crackers,
Out goes you!

Engine, engine number nine,
Going down Chicago line.
If the train falls off the track,
Do you want your money back?
"Yes" (or "No").
Y-E-S (N-O) spells yes (no) and
You are not it!

Jump-Rope Rhymes

Jump-rope rhymes, with their steady beat, often make use of nonsense words and rhyme patterns. Many of the rhymes we provide here are used also with ball bouncing.

I went downtown and met Miss Brown.
She gave me a nickel, I bought a pickle.
The pickle was sour, I bought a flower.
The flower was red, I bought some thread.
The thread was thin, I bought a pin.
The pin was sharp, I bought a harp.
And on that harp I played . . .

(This rhyme is used as a lead-in to any other rhyme.)

This is the way you
spell Tennessee:
One a-see
Two a-see
Three a-see
Four a-see *(etc. to Ten a-see)*

Cinderella, dressed in yellow,
Went upstairs to kiss her fellow.
How many kisses did she get?
1, 2, 3, 4, 5, . . .

Cinderella, dressed in pink,
Washed her dishes in the kitchen sink.
How many dishes did she break?
1, 2, 3, 4, 5, . . .

Cinderella, dressed in red,
Went downtown to get some bread.
How many loaves did she buy?
1, 2, 3, 4, 5, . . .

School, school,
The Golden Rule,
Spell your name
And go to school.

(Child spells name and runs out.)

Apples, peaches, pears and plums,
Tell me when your birthday comes.
January, February, March . . .
First, second, third . . .

(Jump in on your birthday month.
Jump out on the date.)

A my name is Alice (Adam),
My husband's (wife's) name is Adam (Alice).
We live in Alabama
And we sell apples.
B my name is Barbara (Bill),
My husband's (wife's) name is Bill
(Barbara).
We live in Boston
And we sell beans.
C my name is . . .

(Children continue to invent each line, using
successive letters of the alphabet.)

One-a-larkey, two-a-larkey, three-a-larkey, tie;
Four-a-larkey, five-a-larkey, make a pudding pie!
Six-a-larkey, seven-a-larkey, eight-a-larkey, why?
Nine-a-larkey, ten-a-larkey, 'cause it's good, oh, my!

Bluebells, cockle shells,
Evie, Ivy, over,
Bluebells, cockle shells,
Evie, Ivy, under,
Bluebells, cockle shells,
Evie, Ivy, out.

Andy, Mandy,
Sugar candy,
Now's the time
To MISS!

(Children run out just before MISS!)

Mother, Mother, I am sick.
Send for the doctor quick, quick, quick!
In came the doctor,
In came the nurse,
In came the lady with the alligator purse.
"Measles," said the doctor.
"Measles," said the nurse.
"Nothing," said the lady with the alligator purse.

Ipsey, Pipsey.
Tell me true.
Who shall I be married to?
A . . . B . . . C . . . D . . .

(Jump rope until you trip on a letter. It is the first letter of your future spouse's name.)

Two, four, six, eight
Meet me at the garden gate.
If you're late, I won't wait.
Two, four, six, eight.

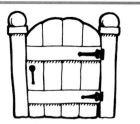

Bubble gum, bubble gum in a dish.
How many pieces do you wish?
1, 2, 3, 4, . . .

Tick tock, tick tock.
Nine o'clock is striking.
Mother, may I go out?
All the kids are waiting.
One has an apple,
One has a bear,
One has a cookie,
One has a dollar, . . .

*(Children continue to invent each line,
using successive letters of the alphabet.)*

Not last night, but the night before
Twenty-four robbers came knockin' at my door.
As I ran out, they ran in.
I hit them on the head with a rolling pin.

Mabel, Mabel,
Set the table.
Don't forget the red, hot, peppers!

*(On the word peppers, those turning
the rope turn it as fast as they can.)*

House to rent,
Enquire within.
When I jump out,
Let _____ jump in.

*(The child jumping calls
the name of a friend to
jump next.)*

Nursery Rhymes

In addition to employing rhyme, the nursery rhymes included in this volume make use of alliteration or nonsensical manipulation of sounds. With a diddlety diddlety, dumpty, a higglety, pigglety, pop, and a clippety clop and hippity hop, children gain an appreciation of sounds. After they have learned these nursery rhymes, children may be encouraged to create their own versions by substituting sounds. Diddlety, diddlety, dumpty may become Riddlety, riddlety, rumpty or Tiddlety, tiddlety, tumpty.

Higglety, Pigglety, Pop!

Higglety, pigglety, pop!
The dog has eaten the mop.
The pig's in a hurry,
The cat's in a flurry,
Higglety, pigglety, pop!

Hickety, Pickety

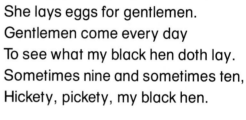

Hickety, pickety, my black hen,
She lays eggs for gentlemen.
Gentlemen come every day
To see what my black hen doth lay.
Sometimes nine and sometimes ten,
Hickety, pickety, my black hen.

Puss up the Plum Tree

Diddlety, diddlety, dumpty,
The cat ran up the plum tree.
Half a crown to fetch her down,
Diddlety, diddlety, dumpty.

Georgie Porgie

Georgie Porgie, pudding and pie,
Kissed the girls and made them cry.
When the boys came out to play,
Georgie Porgie ran away.

Giddy Up

Giddy up horsey,
Don't say stop,
Just let your feet
Go clippety clop.
Clippety clop and hippity hop;
Giddy up,
We're homeward bound.

Rumpty-Iddity

Rumpty-iddity, row, row, row,
If I had a good supper,
I could eat it now.

One Misty, Moisty Morning

One misty, moisty morning,
When cloudy was the weather,
There I met an old man
Clothed all in leather;
Clothed all in leather,
With cap under his chin.
How do you do, and how do you do,
And how do you do again!

Jack-a-Dandy

Nauty Pauty Jack-a-Dandy
Stole a piece of sugar candy
From the grocer's shoppy-shop
And away did hoppy-hop.

The Merchants of London

Hey diddle dinkety, poppety, pet,
The merchants of London they wear scarlet.
Silk in the collar and gold in the hem,
So merrily march the merchant men.

Echo Chants

In these silly chants, the teacher says a line and children repeat the line. This requires good listening, particularly when there is a long, nonsensical line! Everyone can keep the beat by alternately slapping their thighs and clapping their hands.

Birdy

Early in the morning,
When I'm fast asleep,
I hear a little birdy
That goes cheep cheep.
Now this little birdy
Has a funny name.
It is…
Auga flauga feega flooga, ishga
nauga neega nooga,
Auga flauga feega flooga birdy!

Boom Chicka Boom

I said a-boom-chick-a-boom!
I said a-boom-chick-a-boom!
I said a-boom-chick-a-rock-a-chick-a-rock-a-chick-a-boom!
Uh-huh!
Oh Yeah!
This time!
We say it!
LOUDER!

Each time the teacher may add a different variation such as:
SOFTER, SLOWER, FASTER, SWEETLY, ANGRILY.

The Sailor

A sailor went to sea, sea, sea,
To see what he could see, see, see.
But all that he could see, see, see,
Was the bottom of the deep, blue sea, sea, sea.

Flea

Flea!
Flea Fly!
Flea Fly Flo!
Vista
Coo-ma-la, Coo-ma-la, Coo-ma-la Vista
Oh no-no, no, not the vista
Eenie, meenie, decimeenie, oo walla walla meenie,
Exa meenie, soll a meenie, oo walla wall!
Beep belly otin doten bo bo ba deaten dotten shhhh!

My Aunt Came Back

More verses may be added to this chant.

My aunt came back
From old Japan,
And brought with her
A big hand fan.
My aunt came back,
From old Algiers,
And brought with her,
A pair of shears.

My aunt came back,
From Holland too,
And brought with her,
A wooden shoe.
My aunt came back,
From Timbucktoo,
And she brought with her,
Some gum to chew.

My aunt came back,
From Niagara Falls,
And brought with her,
Some ping-pong balls.
My Aunt came back,
From the New York Fair,
And brought with her,
A rocking chair.

My aunt came back,
From Kalamazoo,
And brought with her,
Some nuts like you!!

Playing with Words

Playing with words and their sounds is not a new idea. Generations of families have passed down tongue twisters, children have spoken Pig Latin with friends, and individuals have interchanged the initial sounds of words to create entertaining spoonerisms. Bringing this verbal play into the classroom helps children think about and manipulate the sounds of the speech stream as they shift their attention from the message to the structure of language.

Tongue Twisters

Tongue twisters are phrases or sentences that are difficult to say fast, usually because of an alliteration or a sequence of nearly similar sounds that involves irregular patterns of sounds. As children giggle and stumble over the sounds in a tongue twister, they are raising their consciousness of the phonological basis of language. Listed here are some common tongue twisters which may be used in whole or in part. Short tongue twisters (or, in some cases, the first lines of longer tongue twisters) are appropriate for younger children; the object is to say them over and over again as quickly as possible.

Swan swam over the sea;
Swim, swan, swim!
Swan swam back again,
Well swum, swan!

Six smart sharks.

Toy boat, toy boat

Betty Botter bought some butter.
"But," she said, "the butter's bitter;
If I put it in my batter,
It will make my batter bitter.
But a bit of better butter—
that would make my batter better."

Sly Sam slurps Sally's soup.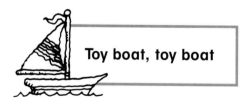

Three free-flow pipes.

Fuzzy Wuzzy was a bear,
Fuzzy Wuzzy had no hair.
Fuzzy Wuzzy wasn't fuzzy,
Was he?

She sees cheese.

Rubber baby-buggy bumpers

A tutor who tooted the flute
Tried to tutor two tooters to toot.
Said the two to their tutor:
"Is it tougher to toot, or
To tutor two tooters to toot?"

Sheep shouldn't sleep in a shack,
Sheep should sleep in a shed.

Peter Piper picked a peck of pickled peppers.
Did Peter Piper pick a peck of pickled peppers?
If Peter Piper picked a peck of pickled peppers,
Where's the peck of pickled peppers Peter Piper picked?

This is a zither.

We surely shall see the sun shine soon.

She says she shall sew a sheet.

Old oily Ollie oils old oily autos.

Billy Button bought a butter biscuit.

Friendly Frank flips fine flapjacks.

Red leather, yellow leather.

Three gray geese in the green grass grazing,
Gray were the geese and green was the grazing.

Six thick thistle sticks.

She sells seashells down by the seashore.

Pig Latin

Pig Latin is an excellent example of manipulation of sounds. The initial sound of each word is deleted and then added to the end of the word with the sound of *ay* added to it. For instance, *nix* becomes *ix-nay, boy* becomes *oy-bay,* teacher becomes *eacher-tay,* and the name *Peter* becomes *Eter-pay.* People who can speak rapid Pig Latin have considerable control over the phonemes of their speech.

Spoonerisms

Spoonerisms are named after the English clergyman William Spooner, who is thought to have made deliberate articulation errors in which initial sounds of words are substituted for one another, as in *With this wing I thee red* or *I'd like a biece of pread.*

Teachers can introduce spoonerisms to children and encourage their attempts to make up their own. A good way to introduce this word play is to use children's names. Invite children to switch the initial sounds in their first and last names. *Randy Jones* becomes *Jandy Rones; Beth Hart* becomes *Heth Bart; Maria Tellez* becomes *Taria Mellez.*

I Spy

In this activity, the teacher selects something in the classroom or on the playground and provides a clue for children to guess the object. Initially, the clue may be a rhyming word. For example, you might say *I spy a meaf.* Children look for an object that rhymes with *meaf* and conclude that the object is a leaf. Provide other clues such as *I spy something green. It is a meaf.* Later, initial sounds may be used as clues: *I spy something that begins with /l/.* As children grow in their ability to think about the sounds in words, give clues that consist of partially or fully segmented words to be blended: *I spy a /l/-/ē f/ or I spy a /l/-/ē/-/f/.*

Activities with Movement

As teachers know, young children enjoy activities in which they can get up and move! In this section, we provide several activities that engage children physically. These activities make use of hand motions or whole-body movements.

Teddy Bear, Teddy Bear

Children perform the actions to this traditional rhyming chant as they recite it. Once children are familiar with this rhyme, encourage them to contribute their own verses. You can suggest a line (e.g., *Teddy Bear, Teddy Bear, touch the sky*) for children to say a corresponding rhyme (e.g, *Teddy Bear, Teddy Bear, wave good-bye!*).

Teddy Bear, Teddy Bear, turn around.
Teddy Bear, Teddy Bear, touch the ground.
Teddy Bear, Teddy Bear, show your shoe.
Teddy Bear, Teddy Bear, that will do.

A Tisket, A Tasket

This game is played in the traditional way, except that the skipping child carries a basket of small objects or picture cards. On the words *I dropped it*, he or she drops an item behind another child in the circle. This child must say a word that rhymes with the name of the object before taking the basket and beginning another round of the game. You might also ask children to segment or delete sounds in a word.

A tisket, a tasket,
A green and yellow basket.
I had a present for my friend,
And on the way I dropped it,
I dropped it,
And on the way, I dropped it.

Bingo

As children sing the lyrics below to the tune of "Bingo," model for them how to progressively replace the syllables in one another's names with a clap. Begin by singing a child's entire name. The next time through the song, clap in place of the first syllable and sing the remaining syllables, and so on until all syllables have been replaced with a clap. Children may use rhythm instruments instead of clapping. The song may also be reversed; children's names may be reconstructed verse by verse. This activity works with any number of syllables. Children with one-syllable names find it humorous to clap only once for their names.

There was a class that had a child
Fernando was his name, oh!
Fer—nan—do! Fer—nan—do! Fer—nan—do!
Fernando was his name, oh!

There was a class that had a child
Fernando was his name, oh!
CLAP—nan-do! CLAP—nan-do! CLAP—nan-do!
Fernando was his name, oh!

There was a class that had a child
Fernando was his name, oh!
CLAP—CLAP-do! CLAP—CLAP-do! CLAP—CLAP-do!
Fernando was his name, oh!

There was a class that had a child
Fernando was his name, oh!
CLAP—CLAP—CLAP! CLAP—CLAP—CLAP! CLAP—CLAP—CLAP!
Fernando was his name, oh!

My Bonnie Lies over the Ocean

As children sing, they move from a sitting to a standing position, or from a standing to a sitting position, each time they say a word beginning with the /b/ sound. The first time through, this song should be sung slowly; increase speed as the children become more and more comfortable with the game.

My Bonnie *(stand)* **lies over the ocean,**
My Bonnie *(sit)* **lies over the sea,**
My Bonnie *(stand)* **lies over the ocean,**
Oh bring *(sit)* **back** *(stand)* **my Bonnie**
  (sit) **to me.**
Bring *(stand)* **back** *(sit)*, **bring** *(stand)*
  back *(sit)*,
Oh bring *(stand)* **back** *(sit)* **my Bonnie**
  (stand) **to me, to me;**
Bring *(sit)* **back** *(stand)*, **bring** *(sit)*
  back *(stand)*,
Oh bring *(sit)* **back** *(stand)* **my Bonnie**
  (sit) **to me.**

Blending Cheer

Make as many words as you wish using the action chant below. In the example, children blend onsets and rimes; however, this cheer may modified to blend compound words, syllables, or phonemes.

Give me a /k/! *(Children repeat /k/ and put*
  up one hand, as in a cheer.)
Give me an /at/! *(Children repeat /at/ and*
  put up the other hand.)
Put them together, *(The teacher and children*
  clap their hands once.)
and we've got a . . . cat! *(Children say* cat
  and wave their hands in the air as they
  say the word.)

Diddle Diddle Dumpling

Have children sit in a circle. One child walks around the outside of the circle while everyone recites the nursery rhyme. On the last line, the child stops. Whoever he or she is standing behind selects a new sound with which to begin the rhyme. If the child selects /k/, the rhyme would begin *Kiddle Kiddle Kumpling*. If the child selects /r/, the rhyme would begin *Riddle Riddle Rumpling*. This child now walks around the outside of the circle as everyone says the new rhyme.

Diddle, diddle, dumpling, my son John,
Went to bed with his trousers on.
One shoe off, and one shoe on,
Diddle, diddle, dumpling, my son John.

Head and Shoulders, Knees and Toes

Sing and perform the actions for this traditional song, replacing the first sound of each word with another sound such as /n/, as presented here.

Ned and noulders, nees and nose,
Nees and nose.
Ned and noulders, nees and nose,
Nees and nose.
Neyes and nears and nead and nose.
Ned and noulders, nees and nose,
NEES AND NOSE!

Using Concrete Objects

Mental process can be made more overt by using objects to represent sounds as they are manipulated. Common objects can be used to support children's emerging linguistic insights.

Stretching Slinkies

A Slinky®, rubber bands, or elastic may be used to demonstrate the stretching and exaggeration of sounds in words. The teacher stretches the prop as he or she elongates a word (e.g., *man becomes mmmmmmmmmaaa-aaaaannnnnnnn*). Children participate in stretching the word. Then the prop is moved back to its original size and everyone says the word in its true form. Because all words have vowel sounds, any word can be stretched. However, some sounds within words cannot be stretched. For instance, the /t/ in *mitt* cannot be stretched, so the word would be elongated as follows: *mmmmmmmiiiiiiiiiiiiiit.*

Interlocking Cubes

Interlocking cubes are ideal for supporting children's understanding of the structure of their language. Cubes can be snapped together as children blend syllables and broken apart as they segment syllables.

For example, say the parts of a word, such as /lol/-/li/-/pop/, and ask children to repeat the parts and pick up a cube for each part they say. In this example, they pick up three cubes, one at a time. Then they snap the cubes together, saying each part and then the entire word. Ask them to put together or break apart other words. Do this same exercise with onsets and rimes (/p/ - /en/) or at the phoneme level (/th/-/u/-/m/ is blended to say *thumb*).

Elkonin Boxes

Designed by the Soviet educator Elkonin, this activity provides children with experience segmenting the phonemes in words. As in the examples that follow, a simple drawing of a word to be analyzed is pictured above a set of boxes equal to the number of phonemes in the word. Children are asked to say the word represented by the picture and to move chips, coins, or counters into the boxes as they slowly say the word. For the first example, as the child slowly articulates the word *fish*, he or she moves a chip into the first box (on the left) and says /f/, a chip into the middle box and says /i/, and a chip into the third box and says the sound /sh/.

(fish)   (mop)

(clock)

(desk)

(nose)

(tree)

Say and Move

A variation of this activity is to have children move a chip representing a given sound into an initial, medial, or final box, depending upon the sound's position in a word. Thus, children are asked to focus on a phoneme's position in a word. For example, the teacher tells children to listen for the /m/ sound in the word *man*. As they repeat the word, they are to move a chip into the first, middle, or final box, depending on the sound's location.

Oo-pples and Boo-noo-noos: Songs and Activities for Phonemic Awareness, Second Edition

Teacher: Say /m/. Listen for the /m/ in this word: *man*.
Where is the /m/ sound in *man*?

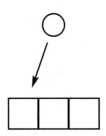

Teacher: Say /t/. Listen for the /t/ in this word: *hat*.
Where is the /t/ sound in *hat*?

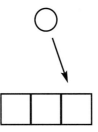

Teacher: Say /u/. Listen for the /u/ in this word: *bus*.
Where is the /u/ sound in *bus*?

Oo-pples and Boo-noo-noos: Songs and Activities for Phonemic Awareness, Second Edition

Using Letters

Although the emphasis in phonemic awareness instruction is on oral language manipulations, several studies indicate that phonemic awareness instruction can be enhanced when letter-sound correspondences are addressed at the same time. Therefore, we include three activities as examples of how letters can be incorporated in phonemic awareness activities.

Willoughby, Wallaby, Woo

The song "Willoughby, Wallaby, Woo" is included in this book and on the accompanying CD. In this song, children's names are sung with a /w/ sound in the initial position before being sung correctly. For example, the name *Justin* is introduced as *Wustin* in the following verse: *Willoughby, Wallaby, Wustin, an elephant sat on Justin.* To add letter representations, print each child's name on a card. Have available a self-stick note with the single letter *W* on it. Hold up each child's name card as you sing about him or her. Place the *W* over the child's initial letter at the appropriate point in the song. Remove the *W* when the child's real name is sung.

You may also wish to change the song to emphasize different sounds. You can sing *Milloughby, Mallaby, Moo* or *Silloughby, Sallaby, Soo* and use the same name cards with the corresponding letters *M* or *S* on self-stick notes.

Scavenger Hunts

Give a small group of children a bag with a letter printed on the outside. Children go on a scavenger hunt around the classroom or search through a collection of items you have placed on a table. They search for objects that begin with the sound represented by the letter on their bag and place the objects inside the bag. After a reasonable period of time, the group displays and tells about the objects in the bag.

Add a Sound

Print a letter on a large card and have children say the sound that it stands for. Children take turns touching classroom objects with the letter card and saying each object's name, adding the sound on the card to the end of the name. For example, if the card has the letter *o* on it, the children would add the /o/ sound to words as they touch objects. Touching a door, a child would say door-o; touching a crayon, he or she would say crayon-o.

This activity can be enriched by reading Altoona Baboona (see page 34) and singing His Four Fur Feet (see page 83), since each has the addition of a sound to the end of words as a dominant feature.

Reading Aloud from Books That Play with Sounds

Read-aloud books can help children develop a sensitivity to the sound structure of language. In the books listed on pages 34–37, play with language is a dominant feature, so children are likely to notice it. The books lend themselves to further, often spontaneous, language play. Children repeat "rock-a-poodle-moo" from Bernard Most's *Cock-a-Doodle-Moo*. They laugh as they twist it and turn it in their mouths, changing it to "sock-a-doodle-soo" and "mock-a-doodle-doo."

Books of this nature should be read over and over again. Encourage children to notice the language use and prompt them to make predictions: "[The slug] went scrass, scrass, scrass through the tall, green . . ." Pause to ask: *What do you think the slug is crawling through?* Children might be asked to explain how they derived their predictions: *What made you think the next word would be* grass? Generally, the answer will address the author's use of language: "She's making the words rhyme!" as in this example from *Rainy Day Slug* by Mary Palenick Colborn.

Follow-up activities can include having children invent another version of a story, compose additional events using the author's patterns, or engage in other activities that follow the patterns found in the book. For example, after listening to Dr. Seuss's *There's a Wocket in My Pocket,* have children draw and name their own unusual creatures. After hearing Arlene Mosel's *Tikki Tikki Tembo,* invite children to clap the syllables of their own and their classmates' names and create graphs of long and short names. After several retellings of *The Animals' Song* by David Harrison, children can act out the story.

Annotated Bibliography

Ahlberg, Janet and Allan. *Each Peach Pear Plum.* **Puffin, 1978.**   In this playful rhyming book, the reader must look carefully at each picture to find a hidden character.

Aylesworth, Jim. *My Son John.* **Henry Holt, 1994.**   With a farm as the setting, Aylesworth creates fourteen new versions of the Mother Goose rhyme "Diddle Diddle Dumpling." The book provides wonderful models for children to develop their own Diddle Diddle Dumpling rhymes.

Bayer, Jane. *A My Name is Alice.* **Dial, 1984.**   Using a familiar alphabet rhyme, the author takes us on an alliterative adventure with animals that sell some unusual items.

Bynam, Janie. *Altoona Baboona.* **Harcourt Brace, 1999.**   After flicking peas with a spoon-a and dancing and singing to the moon-a, Altoona Baboona gets bored on her sand dune-a and decides to seek adventure in a hot air balloon-a. Children will be adding sounds to words all day long-a.

Clements, Andrew. *Double Trouble in Walla Walla.* **Scholastic, 1997.**   What began as an ordinary day in Walla Walla quickly turns into one of trouble as Lulu finds herself using unusual "double" words such as *nit-wit, higgledy-piggledy,* and *mish-mash.*

Colborn, Mary. *Rainy Day Slug.* **Sasquatch, 2000.**   A slug leaves its garden to scrass, scrass, scrass through the grass; scuddle scuddle scuddle through a puddle; scrack scrack scrack through a crack until it makes its way into the bedroom of a young child.

Degen, Bruce. *Daddy Is a Doodlebug.* **HarperCollins, 2000.**   A young doodlebug describes the things he and his father enjoy doodling together: eating potoodle chips, walking their poodlebug down the lane, riding the caboodle car on the train, and many more "oodle" activities.

Degan, Bruce. *Jamberry.* **HarperCollins, 1983.**   A boy and a bear have wonderful adventures in a land of berries. The engaging, rhyming and rhythmical text uses the word *berry* in creative ways: *Hatberry, shoeberry, in my canoeberry* and *Quickberry! Quackberry! Pick me a blackberry!*

Dunn, Opal. *Acka Backa BOO! Playground Games from Around the World.* **Henry Holt, 2000.**   The author shares a collection of games from around the world that are accompanied by simple rhymes.

Edwards, Pamela Duncan. *The Worrywarts.* **HarperCollins, 1999.**   Wombat, Weasel, and Woodchuck set out to wander the world one Wednesday. Taking with them items such as walnut wafers, waffles with whipped cream, wieners, a walking stick, and the *W* volume of *Webster's Book of Words*, the trio sets off— but not without worrying about the possible dangers of wasps, wolves, and worked-up owls attacking. This whimsical tale is filled with words beginning with /w/!

Fleming, Denise. *Barnyard Banter.* **Henry Holt, 1994.**   Using a rhyming format, this simple book shares the sights and sounds of a barnyard. Cows moo, moo, moo and roosters cock-a-doodle doo; hens cluck, cluck, cluck while pigs wallow in the muck, muck, muck.

Florian, Douglas. *Laugh-eteria.* **Harcourt Brace, 1999.**   Many poems in this collection can be used to support phonemic awareness development. Favorites include "Hello, My Name is Dracula," in which Dracula wears blackula, drives a Cadillacula and is a maniacula and "Pizza Treatsa," in which the speaker loves to eatsa pizza with hands or feetsa.

Garcia, Jerry and Grisman, David. *What Will You Wear, Jenny Jenkins?* **HarperCollins, 2000.** Jennie Jenkins's mother tries to help her decide what to wear in this song-put-to-text. Jennie Jenkins won't wear white because the color's too bright; blue is too true, yellow won't get her a fellow, and beige shows her age. After considering other colors, she finally says, *Oh what do you care, if I just go bare?* and Jennie Jenkins, a little bear, heads off. In addition to the rhyme feature, this song includes silly nonsense phrases.

Guarino, Deborah. *Is Your Mama a Llama?* **Scholastic, 1991.** In this book of riddles and rhyme, a young llama asks a variety of animals if their mamas are llamas. Each one replies with a description of its mama and concludes that its mama could not be a llama. When the reader turns the page, the identity of its mother is revealed.

Guthrie, Woody. *Howdi Do.* **Candlewick, 2000.** Woody Guthrie's wonderful, tongue twisting, laugh-out-loud song "Howdi Do" is illustrated by Vladimir Radunsky in this book.

Harrison, David L. *The Animals' Song.* **Boyds Mills, 1997.** With a tweet tweet tweetity tweet, a hoot hoot hootity hoot, a yip yap yippity yap, and more, animals join a girl playing her flute, toot toot tootity toot, on a musical parade. What ensues is a marvelous cacophony of sound!

Hudson, Wade and Cheryl. *How Sweet the Sound: African-American Songs for Children.* **Scholastic, 1995.** The authors share the lyrics and scores from several African-American songs including spirituals, work songs, play songs, and chants. Many of the selections make use of rhyme and repetition. Others make use of alliteration and phoneme manipulation.

Jonas, Ann. *Watch William Walk.* **Greenwillow, 1997.** In this alliterative adventure, William and Wilma go for a walk on the beach with Wally the dog and Wanda the duck. The author-illustrator provides an aerial view of the characters' adventures.

Lear, Edward. *A Was Once an Apple Pie.* **Candlewick, 1997.** This engaging alphabet book encourages children to play with the sounds of their language as the letters A to Z are introduced in a rhythmical and nonsensical way: *A was once an apple pie, Pidy Widy Tidy Pidy/Nice insidy Apple pie.* Each letter follows the same predictable pattern.

London, Jonathan. *Snuggle Wuggle.* **Scholastic, 2000.** Just as human mothers hug their children, so do animal mothers! Using a rhyming pattern, the book shares a variety of ways animals hug: Bunnies snuggle wuggle, otters tumble bumble, and so on.

Kroll, Virginia. *Jaha and Jamil Went down the Hill: An African Mother Goose.* **Charlesbridge, 1995.** Using Mother Goose verses as models, the author shares rhymes that reflect some of the customs of both modern and traditional African life.

Mosel, Arlene. *Tikki Tikki Tembo.* **Henry Holt, 1989.** Tikki Tikki Tembo No Sa Rembo Chari Bari Ruchi Pip Peri Pembo is a boy whose mother gave him his great long name because he is the first-born son in the family. His younger, and therefore less important, brother is named Chang. One day Tikki Tikki Tembo falls into a well, but because of his great long name, communicating the problem and getting assistance take considerable time.

**Most, Bernard. *Cock-a-Doodle-Moo!*
Harcourt Brace, 1996.** A rooster wakes up one morning to discover that he cannot crow above a whisper. He tries desperately to teach the cow to say *Cock-a-doodle-doo* so that she can awaken the farm animals. The cow struggles with this task, substituting sounds in the wake-up call in many ways. She says *Mock-a-moodle-moo!* and *Rock-a-poodle-moo!* but she just cannot say Cock-a-doodle-doo. When she gets close enough—with *Cock-a-doodle-moo!*—the rooster encourages her to awaken the farm animals.

Pomerantz, Charlotte. *The Piggy in the Puddle.* Aladdin, 1974. A little pig is having a delightful time playing in a mud puddle. Her disapproving father (*fuddy-duddy, fuddy-duddy, fuddy-duddy*), mother (*fiddle-faddle, fiddle-faddle, fiddle-faddle*) and brother (*silly billy, silly billy, silly billy*) try to persuade her to get out. Unable to persuade the wiggling, giggling little pig to leave the squishy-squashy, mooshy-squooshy puddle, her family decides to join her!

Root, Phyllis. *Foggy Friday.* Candlewick, 2000. Reminiscent of the rooster in Bernard Most's *Cock-a-Doodle Moo!*, the rooster in this book loses his voice and cannot awaken the farm. Other animals attempt to help and the phoneme play begins as the pig cries, *Oink-a-oodle-oo!* The cow tries *Moo-a-moodle-moo!* and the chicks say *Cheep-a-choodle-choo!*

Rosen, Michael. *We're Going on a Bear Hunt.* Little Simon, 1997. In this rhythmical book, a family goes on a bear hunt. The father, mother, and three children make their way through long, wavy grass (*swishy, swashy*), a deep, cold river (*splash, splosh*), and other exciting, scary, noisy places before they come to a narrow, gloomy cave. They're not afraid—until they see a bear! They race back home, jump into bed together, and pull the covers over their heads.

Seuss, Dr. *Fox in Socks.* Random House, 1965. Before beginning this book, the reader is warned to read slowly because the fox will try to get the reader's tongue in trouble. The play with language is the very obvious focus, with assonance patterns, vowel sound changes, and clever language play.

Seuss, Dr. *There's a Wocket in My Pocket.* Random House, 1974. A child talks about the creatures he has found in various locations in his house. These include a *nooth grush on my toothbrush* and a *zamp in the lamp*. The initial sounds of common household objects are substituted with other sounds to make the nonsense creatures.

Shaw, Nancy. *Sheep in a Jeep.* Houghton Mifflin, 1986. Five sheep have an adventure in a jeep that gets stuck in the mud. The book is filled with rhyme, with an emphasis on words that rhyme with *sheep: jeep, steep, leap, deep,* and *more.*

Shields, Carol D. *Animagicals:* Music. Handprint, 1999. Using rhythm, rhyme and nonsense play with sounds, the author provides clues to the identity of 12 animals in this book of fold-out pages.

Slate, Joseph. *Miss Bindergarten Gets Ready for Kindergarten.* Dutton, 1996. In this rhyming alphabet book, Miss Bindergarten prepares her classroom for a new school year. We also meet 26 children, with names beginning from *A* to *Z*, preparing for their first day of kindergarten. This book and its companion, *Miss Bindergarten Celebrates the 100th Day of Kindergarten,* are delightful books to share with preschoolers and kindergarteners.

Waber, Bernard. *Bearsie Bear and the Surprise Sleepover Party.* Houghton Mifflin, 1997. Bearsie Bear is just falling asleep inside his warm cabin one winter night when he hears a knock at the door. It is Moosie Moose, hoping for shelter from the cold night. Bearsie Bear lets Moosie Moose in and, with a "Hooray!" Moosie Moose jumps into bed. Soon there is another knock at the door. This time it is Cowsie Cow who also wants to come in for the night. Eventually they are joined by Piggie Pig, Foxie Fox, Goosie Goose, and Porkie Porcupine. The repetition of the playful names lends humor to this entertaining tale.

Wishinsky, Frieda. *Oonga Boonga.* Dutton, 1998. To no avail, the family and neighbors of an infant go to great lengths to stop her uncontrollable crying. Only Brother Daniel, with his *oonga boonga* and *bunka bunka*, is able to calm her.

Yolen, Jane. *Off We Go!* Little, Brown, 2000. With a tip-toe, tippity toe, hip-hop, hippity hop, dig-deep, diggity deep, and slither-slee, slithery slee, a mouse, frog, mole, and snake (along with other animals who make their own special noises) travel to Grandma's house. This short, simple, beautifully illustrated book will inspire children to mimic and manipulate sounds!

Poems That Play with Sounds

Enrich children's literacy experiences by reading poetry aloud often. Share their delight as they discover how poets create nonsense words and make use of alliteration, tongue twisters, and rhyme. Entice them with poems that employ unusual and unexpected combinations of sounds. Give them daily experiences with poetry to hear poets manipulating language and the sounds of language.

As children listen to the sounds in Jack Prelutsky's repeated refrain *yickity-yackity, yickity-yak,* hear about Margaret Wise Brown's *rumbly, tumbly, bumbly bee,* and note that Douglas Florian loves to *eatsa chewy pizza,* they experience the lively and rollicking manipulation of sounds poets use to entertain and amuse. They want to chime in when they hear *Dig dig digging dirt, digging dirt is best.*

The poems offered here are ones that exploit sounds; their rhythm and their play with sounds is not subtle. Share these poems at any time. Read them aloud, over and over again. Always invite children to join in. Encourage their participation in poetry!

ANKYLOSAURUS

All covered with armor the *Ankylosaurus*
Moved with a clunk and a *Clankylosaurus.*
He stood in a stream as he *Drankylosaurus*
And looked like an old army *Tankylosaurus.*

Of course, to be perfectly *Frankylosaurus,*
He had quite a low dino *Rankylosaurus.*
His small mind was often a *Blankylosaurus.*
His smell? Sad to say it, he *Stankylosaurus.*

When down by the old river *Bankylosaurus,*
His young brother's tail he would *Yankylosaurus,*
And this naughty dinosaur *Prankylosaurus*
Might well cause his parents to *Spankylosaurus.*

Time passed and his high spirits *Sankylosaurus*
As dinosaur numbers all *Shrankylosaurus.*
So now I'll say bye-bye and *Thankylosaurus*
'Cause that's all I know about *Ankylosaurus.*

Jeff Moss

Baby's Drinking Song

Sip a little
Sup a little
From your little
Cup a little
Sup a little
Sip a little
Put it to your
Lip a little
Tip a little
Tap a little
Not into your
Lap or it'll
Drip a little
Drop a little
On the table
Top a little.

James Kirkup

(This poem has to be read aloud three times—each time faster than the last.)

• • • • • • • • •

BUMBLE BEE

Black and yellow
Little fur bee
Buzzing away
In the timothy
Drowsy
Browsy
Lump of a bee
Rumbly
Tumbly
Bumbly bee.
Where are you taking
Your golden plunder
Humming along
Like baby thunder?
Over the clover
And over the hay
Then over the apple trees
Zoom away.

Margaret Wise Brown

THE BLUFFALO

Oh, do not tease the Bluffalo
With quick-step or with shuffalo
When you are in a scuffalo
In Bluffalo's backyard.

For it has quite enoughalo
Of people playing toughalo
And when it gives a cuffalo
It gives it very hard.

But if by chance a scuffalo
Occurs twixt you and Bluffalo,
Pray tempt it with a truffalo
And catch it off its guard.

And while it eats that stuffalo
You can escape the Bluffalo
And with a huff and puffalo
Depart from its backyard.

Jane Yolen

Clickbeetle

Click beetle
Clack beetle
Snapjack black beetle
Glint glitter glare beetle
Pin it in your hair beetle
Tack it to your shawl beetle
Wear it at the ball beetle
Shine shimmer spark beetle
Glisten in the dark beetle
Listen to it crack beetle
Click beetle
Clack beetle

Mary Ann Hoberman

THE DIGGING SONG

In your hands you hold the spade,
Feel its well worn wood.
Now you drive it in the earth,
Drive it deep and good.

    Dig dig digging dirt,
    Dirt inside your vest.
    Dig dig digging dirt,
    Digging dirt is best.

Soon your hands are red and raw,
Blisters on the way,
But your spade just wants to dig
All the long, hot day.

    Dig dig digging dirt,
    Dirt inside your vest.
    Dig dig digging dirt,
    Digging dirt is best.

Wes Magee

Cricket

Black   shiny
Crickety   cricket,
Hop   quick
Quickety   quicket.

My   cat   is   ready
To   springety   spring.
Jump   quick,
Crickety   cricketing   thing.

Leap   to   a   small   crooked
Crackety   crack.
Squeezy   squeeze in,
And   don't   scroodge   back.

James Tippett

The Diners in the Kitchen

Our dog Fred
Et the bread

Our dog Dash
Et the hash

Our dog Pete
Et the meat

Our dog Davy
Et the gravy

Our dog Toffy
Et the coffee

And—the worst
From the first—

Our dog Fido
Et the pie-dough.

James Whitcomb Riley

• • • • • • • • • •

Do-It-Yourself Poem

I didn't have time to finish this poem,
So you can write it on your _____.
Fill in a word, a rhyme or two.
It isn't very hard to _____.
Keep the rhythm and the beat.
Keep each sentence short and _____.
Now, at last, this poem must end.
Thank you very much, my _____.

Douglas Florian

• • • • • • • • • •

Ducks

Daphne Duck and Daisy Duck,
Diggory, Dee, and Jim,
Went down to the duck pond
To see if they could swim.
Daphne could, and Daisy could,
And Diggory could, and Dee—
But Jim sank to the bottom.
Oh, dear me.

Kaye Umansky

• Point to each finger
  in turn.

• Walk fingers along.

• Swim with hand.

• Turn thumb upside down
  and shake head.

Eletelephony

Once there was an elephant,
Who tried to use the telephant—
No! no! I mean an elephone
Who tried to use the telephone—
(Dear me! I am not certain quite
That even now I've got it right.)

Howe'er it was, he got his trunk
Entangled in the telephunk;
The more he tried to get it free,
The louder buzzed the telephee—
(I fear I'd better drop the song
of elephop and telephong!)

Laura E. Richards

• • • • • • • • • •

Fish

Look at them flit
Lickety-split
Wiggling
Swiggling
Swerving
Curving
Hurrying
Scurrying
Chasing
Racing
Whizzing
Whisking
Flying
Frisking
Tearing around
With a leap and a bound
But none of them making the tiniest

tiniest

tiniest

tiniest

sound.

Mary Ann Hoberman

• • • • • • • • • •

Froggie

Froggie, froggie.
Hippity-hop!
When you get to the sea
You do not stop.
Plop!

Anonymous

Galoshes

Susie's galoshes
Make splishes and sploshes
And slooshes and sloshes
As Susie steps slowly
Along in the slush.

They stamp and they tramp
On the ice and concrete,
They get stuck in the muck and the mud;
But Susie likes much best to hear

The slippery slush
As it slooshes and sloshes,
And splishes and sploshes,
All around her galoshes!

Rhoda Bacmeister

Give Me a Pancake

Tippety, tippety tin,
Give me a pancake and I will come in.
Tippety, tippety toe,
Give me a pancake and I will go.

Anonymous

• • • • • • • • • •

Hippopotamus

See the handsome hippopotamus,
Wading on the river-bottomus.
He goes everywhere he wishes
In pursuit of little fishes.
Cooks them in his cooking-potamus.
"My," fish say, "he eats a lot-of-us!"

Joanna Cole

Habits of the Hippopotamus

The hippopotamus is strong
    And huge of head and broad of bustle;
The limbs on which he rolls along
    Are big with hippopotomuscle.

He does not greatly care for sweets
    Like ice cream, apple pie, or custard,
But takes to flavor what he eats
    A little hippopotomustard.

The hippopotamus is true
    To all his principles, and just;
He always tries his best to do
    The things one hippopotomust.

He never rides in trucks or trams,
    In taxicabs or omnibuses,
And so keeps out of traffic jams
    And other hippopotomusses.

Arthur Guiterman

Is It Possicle?

There once was a sweet little Mousicle
   (An especially good kind of mouse),
Who lived with his friend in a housicle
   (An especially good kind of house).
   He rode a bicycle,
   She rode a tricycle,
Exactly the size for the mice.
On Sunday they feasted on strawberry icicle.
Strawberry icicle's awfully nicicle.
   (And nicicle's nicer than nice.)

Marion Edey

. . . .

If Your Car Goes

If your car goes *clippety-clump*
Each time it hits a bippety-bump,
And on a turn you hear a *clunk*—
A clinking, clanking, clunking *plunk*—
Maybe . . .
A turtle's hiding in your trunk.

Douglas Florian

ICKLY PRICKLY PORCUPINE

Ickly prickly porcupine,
Her back is full of prickles—(ouch)
Turn her over gently
And give her tummy tickles—(ah)

Kaye Umansky

- **Make prickly shape
  with hands.**

- **Turn hands over and
  tickle palm.**

Keep Your Eyes

Keep your eyes
Off my fries.
Keep your knees
Off my peas.
Keep your belly
Off my jelly.
Keep your hair
Off my pear.
Keep your legs
Off my eggs.
And *please,* keep your brain
Off my chow mein.

Douglas Florian

Lily Lee

I like Lily,
Little Lily Lee;
I like Lily
And Lily likes me.
Lily likes lollipops,
Lemonade and lime-drops,
But I like Lily,
Little Lily Lee.

Isobel Best

Moses and His Toeses

Moses supposes his toeses are roses,
But Moses supposes erroneously,
For nobody's toeses we knowses are roses,
As Moses supposes his toeses to be!

Traditional

The Last Cry of the Damp Fly

Bitter batter boop!
I'm swimming in your soup.

Bitter batter bout;
Kindly get me out!

Bitter batter boon:
Not upon your spoon!

Bitter batter bum!
Now I'm in your tum!

Dennis Lee

Oodles of Noodles

I love noodles. Give me oodles.
Make a mound up to the sun.
Noodles are my favorite foodles.
I eat noodles by the ton.

Lucia and James L. Hymes, Jr.

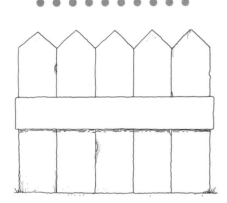

Pizza Treatsa

I love to eatsa
Chewy pizza,
Standing up
Or in a seatsa.
A neatsa pizza
Can't be beatsa.
Eat it with your
Hands or feetsa.

Douglas Florian

The Pickety Fence

The pickety fence
The pickety fence
Give it a lick it's
The pickety fence
Give it a lick it's
A clickety fence
Give it a lick it's
A lickety fence
Give it a lick
Give it a lick
Give it a lick
With a rickety stick
Pickety
Pickety
Pickety
Pick

David McCord

Snakes

Snakes are slender.
Snakes are sleek.
Snakes like playing
Hide-and-seek.

Snakes are sneaky.
Snakes are sly.
Snakes will look you
In the eye.

Snakes are clever.
Snakes are fast.
If you see one
Let it pass.

Charles Ghigna

There Was a Little Dog

There was a little dog, and he had a little tail.
  And he used to wag, wag, wag it.
But whenever he was sad because he had been bad,
  On the ground he would drag, drag, drag it.

He had a little nose, as of course you would suppose,
  And on it was a muz-muz-muzzle,
And to get it off he'd try till a tear stood in his eye,
  But he found it a puz-puz-puzzle.

Anonymous

• • • • • • • • • • •

The Tiger

I am a cat—come hear me purrrr.
I've many stripes upon my furrrr.
I speed through forests like a blurrrr.
I hunt at night—I am tigerrrr.

Douglas Florian

• • • • • • • • • • •

The Washing Machine

Dirty clothes will soon get clean
If you pop them in the washing machine.
And the clothes go around and around,
And the clothes go around.
They'll be done in the wink of an eye,
Then we'll hang them out to dry.
And the clothes go flip, flap, flop!
And the clothes go flip, flap, flop!

Kaye Umansky

• Revolve arms in circular motion.

• Flop arms alternately up and down.

Weather

Dot a dot dot   dot a dot dot
Spotting the windowpane.
Spack a spack speck   flick a flack fleck
Freckling the windowpane.

A spatter a scatter   a wet cat a clatter
A splatter a rumble outside.
Umbrella umbrella umbrella umbrella
Bumbershoot barrel of rain.

Slosh a galosh   slosh a galosh
Slither and slather a glide
A puddle a jump a puddle a jump
A puddle a jump puddle splosh
A juddle a pump aluddle a dump a
Puddmuddle jump in and slide!

Eve Merriam

Whisky
Frisky

Whisky frisky,
Hippity hop,
Up he goes
To the tree top!

Whirly, twirly,
Round and round,
Down he scampers
To the ground.

Furly, curly,
What a tail,
Tall as a feather,
Broad as a sail.

Where's his supper?
In the shell.
Snappy, cracky,
Out it fell.

Anonymous

Wiggly Giggles

I've got the wiggly-wiggles today,
And I just can't sit still.
My teacher says she'll have to find
A stop-me-wiggle pill.

I've got the giggly-giggles today;
I couldn't tell you why.
But if Mary hiccups one more time
I'll giggle till I cry.

I've got to stamp my wiggles out
And hold my giggles in,
Cause wiggling makes me giggle
And gigglers never win.

*Stacy Jo Crossen and
Natalie Anne Covell*

Words That Describe the Eating Habits of Two Dinosaurs and My Cousin

Carnivorous means that you eat only meat
Like the gigantic fearsome *T. rex.*
Herbivorous means that you eat only plants
Like the brachiosaurs with long necks.
But I've got a word to describe Cousin Pete
Whose strange eating habits arise—
Frenchfrivorous tells you about what he'll eat,
Since all that he eats is french fries.

Jeff Moss

The Yak

Yickity-yackity, yickity-yak,
the yak has a scriffily, scraffily back;
some yaks are brown yaks and some yaks are black,
yickity-yackity, yickity-yak.

Sniggildy-snaggildy, sniggildy-snag,
the yak is all covered with shiggildy-shag;
he walks with a ziggildy-zaggildy-zag,
sniggildy-snaggildy, sniggildy-snag.

Yickity-yackity, yickity-yak,
the yak has a scriffily, scraffily back;
some yaks are brown and some yaks are black,
yickity-yackity, yickity-yak.

Jack Prelutsky

Songs That Play with Sounds

Most young children love to sing, especially songs in which they take an active part. Many songs encourage experimentation with and manipulation of language through alliteration, rhyme, or phoneme substitution or addition. Songs that make use of nonsensical combinations of sounds draw children's attention to the sounds rather than the meaning of the lyrics. Sing daily! Play the CD at different times. Help children learn the songs, and talk about why they are fun to sing.

Some songs beg for more verses. Once children have discovered the rhyme pattern in "Down by the Bay," for example, you can model how to make up a new verse and prompt children to do the same: *Let's make up a new verse about a snake. How about "Did you ever see a snake working with a rake?"* Encourage children to create more verses for:

- "A-Hunting We Will Go"
- "Barnyard Song"
- "Circus Parade"
- "The Corner Grocery Store"
- "The Name Game"

Some songs are well suited for phoneme substitution. Once children are comfortable with the original lyrics, encourage them to change some sounds. What other sound could be added to the end of words in "His Four Fur Feet" or "The Fox"? What other sound could be used in the middle of the nonsense in "The Bee and the Pup"?

Help children find the silly strings of sounds in these songs and change the initial, medial, or final phoneme:

- "I've Been Working on the Railroad"
- "The Old Gray Horse"
- "Old Molly Hare"
- "Frog Went a-Courtin'"
- "The Happy Wanderer"

Make all of these songs part of your phonemically rich classroom!

Planning Guide

This chart lists each of the songs included in this book and the accompanying CD, identified by type of phonemic manipulation.

Song	Rhyme	Alliteration	Phoneme Substitution	Phoneme Addition	Nonsense Manipulation
A-Hunting We Will Go	●				
Apples and Bananas			●		
Barnyard Song	●	●			●
The Bee and the Pup	●			●	
Burgalesa	●			●	
Chickery Chick	●	●			●
Circus Parade					●
Clickety-Clack	●		●		
The Corner Grocery Store	●				
Down by the Bay	●				
Fingers, Nose, and Toes	●				
Fooba-Wooba John	●		●		●
The Fox	●			●	
Frog Went A-Courtin'	●				
Goin' to the Zoo	●	●	●		
The Happy Wanderer	●		●		●
His Four Fur Feet		●		●	
Howdido	●	●	●		●

Oo-pples and Boo-noo-noos: Songs and Activities for Phonemic Awareness, Second Edition

Song	Rhyme	Alliteration	Phoneme Substitution	Phoneme Addition	Nonsense Manipulation
Hush, Little Baby	●				
I Make Myself Welcome	●	●			●
I've Been Working on the Railroad	●	●	●		●
Jennie Jenkins	●	●	●		●
Jim Along, Josie		●			
Kicklety Kacklety	●	●	●		●
Kitty Alone	●	●			●
Little Sacka Sugar		●	●		●
Michael Finnegan	●			●	
The Name Game	●	●	●	●	●
The Old Gray Horse	●	●			●
Old Molly Hare	●	●	●		●
Pounding a Nail	●	●	●		●
Raindrops	●	●	●		
She'll Be Comin' Round the Mountain When She Comes		●			
This Old Man	●		●		●
Too-ra-ray					●
Whosery Here?	●			●	
Willoughby, Wallaby, Woo	●	●	●		
Zany Zaddlepate	●	●			●

A-Hunting We Will Go

Brightly

English Folk Song

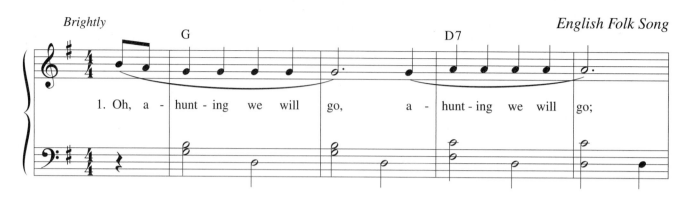

1. Oh, a - hunt - ing we will go, a - hunt - ing we will go;

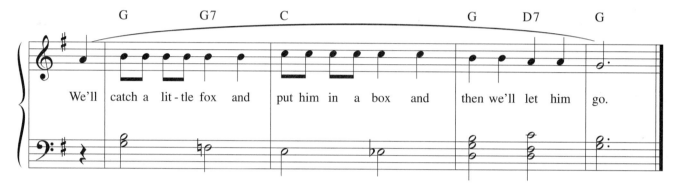

We'll catch a lit - tle fox and put him in a box and then we'll let him go.

2. We'll catch a little squirrel and give it to a girl.

3. We'll catch a little dog and put it on a log.

4. We'll catch a little fish and put it in a dish.

5. We'll catch a little mouse and take it in the house.

6. We'll catch a little pig and make it do a jig.

Apples and Bananas

Traditional
Arranged by John Sauls, Jr.

1. I like to eat, eat, eat, Ap-ples and ba-nan-as; I like to eat, eat, eat, Ap-ples and ba-nan-as.

1. I like to
2.

2. I like to ate, ate, ate,
   Ape-ples and ba-nay-nays;
   I like to ate, ate, ate,
   Ape-ples and ba-nay-nays;

3. I like to eat, eat, eat,
   Ee-pples and bee-nee-nees;
   I like to eat, eat, eat,
   Ee-pples and bee-nee-nees;

4. I like to ite, ite, ite,
   I-pples and bi-ni-nis;
   I like to ite, ite, ite,
   I-pples and bi-ni-nis;

5. I like to oat, oat, oat,
   O-pples and bo-no-nos;
   I like to oat, oat, oat,
   O-pples and bo-no-nos;

6. I like to oot, oot, oot,
   Oo-pples and boo-noo-noos;
   I like to oot, oot, oot,
   Oo-pples and boo-noo-noos;

Repeat first verse.

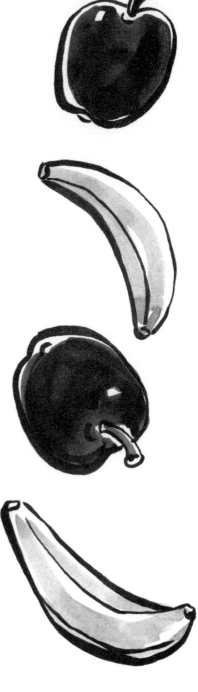

BARNYARD SONG

Kentucky Mountain Folk Song

1. I had a cat, and the cat pleased me; I fed my cat by yon-der
2. I had a hen, and the hen pleased me; I fed my hen by yon-der
3. I had a duck, and the duck pleased me; I fed my duck by yon-der

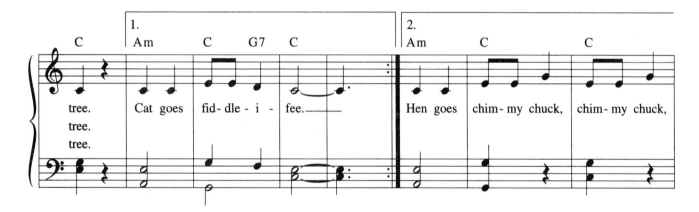

tree. Cat goes fid-dle-i-fee.
tree.
tree.

Hen goes chim-my chuck, chim-my chuck,

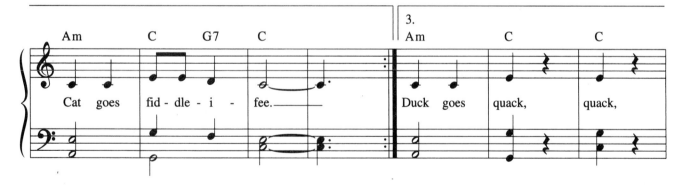

Cat goes fid-dle-i-fee.

Duck goes quack, quack,

Hen goes chim-my chuck, chim-my chuck, Cat goes fid-dle-i-fee.

Add more verses by using goose, sheep, hog, cow, horse, and dog.

The Bee and the Pup

Traditional

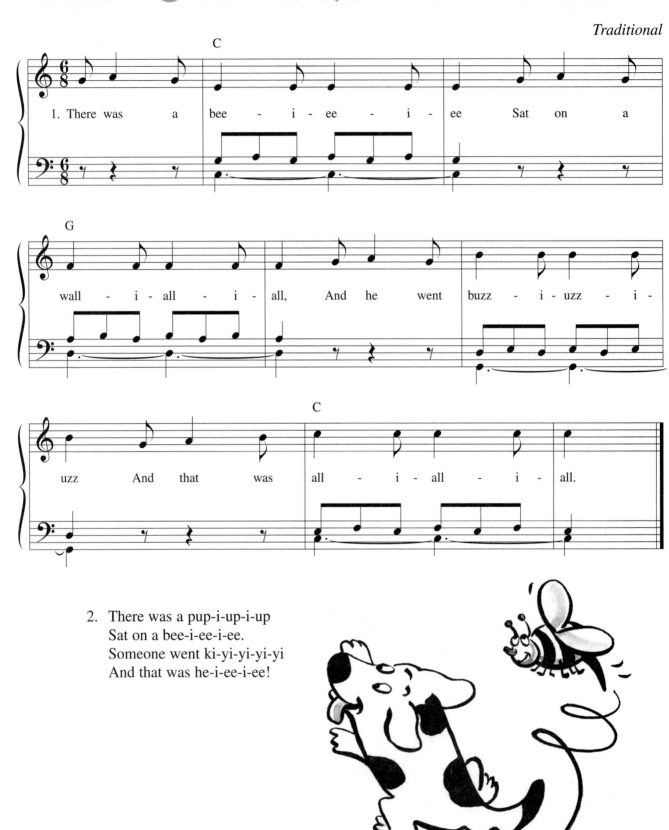

2. There was a pup-i-up-i-up
   Sat on a bee-i-ee-i-ee.
   Someone went ki-yi-yi-yi-yi
   And that was he-i-ee-i-ee!

Burgalesa

Folk Song from Spain
Arranged by John Sauls, Jr.

Moderately

1. I have two bill - i - rills, Two dol - lar bill - i - rills, And twen - ty nick - el - els That I can spend, I have a
2. There's a fi - es - ta - ra, Such a fi - es - ta - ra, Down at the pla - za - ra, I'll take you there, For this fi -

cart - a - ra,   Such a fine cart - a - ra,   Drawn by a
es - ta - ra's,   A grand fi - es - ta - ra,   The ver - y

mule - a - ra,   Hop in,   my   friend.
best - a - ra,   found   an - y   where.

Chickery Chick

Words by Sylvia Dee
Music by Sidney Lippman

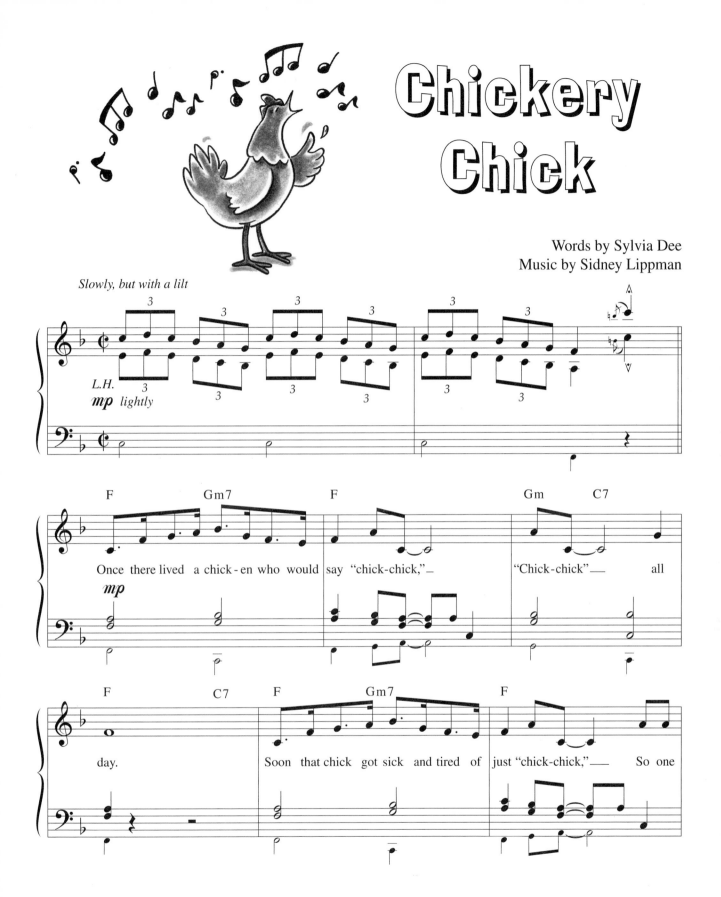

Slowly, but with a lilt

Once there lived a chick-en who would say "chick-chick,"— "Chick-chick"—— all day. Soon that chick got sick and tired of just "chick-chick,"—— So one

CIRCUS PARADE

Words and Music by Milton Kaye

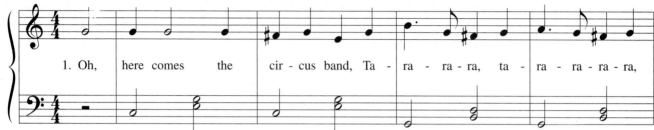

1. Oh, here comes the cir - cus band, Ta - ra - ra - ra, ta - ra - ra - ra - ra,

Here comes the cir - cus band, Ta - ra - ra - ra - ra - ra!

Refrain

Zing! Zing!_____ Zing! Zing!_____

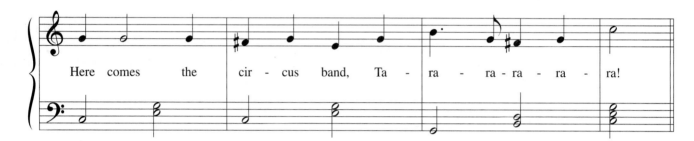

Ta - ra - ra - ra, Ta - ra - ra - ra.

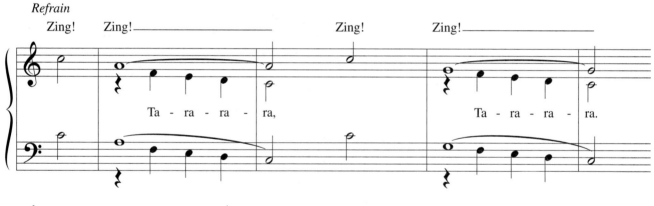

Oh, how much I love the cir - cus, Ta - ra - ra! Boom! Boom!

2. Oh, here come the elephants,
   Clump-clump-ta-ra, clump-clump-ta-ra-ra,
   Here come the elephants,
   Clump-clump-ta-ra-ra-ra. *Refrain*

3. Oh, here come the merry clowns,
   Ha-ha-ta-ra, ha-ha-ta-ra-ra,
   Here come the merry clowns,
   Ha-ha-ta-ra-ra-ra. *Refrain*

4. Oh, here come the dancing bears,
   Thump-thump-ta-ra, thump-thump-ta-ra-ra,
   Here come the dancing bears,
   Thump-thump-ta-ra-ra-ra. *Refrain*

CLICKETY-CLACK

Words and Music by Charles Harvey

1. Click-et-y-clack, a-lunk, a-lunk! A train is com-ing, a-chunck, a-chunck; A
2. O-ver the bridge, a-cross the lake, A mile a min-ute it has to make; A

click-et-y-clack a mile a-way; It has-n't a sec-ond o' time to stay; It
ter-ri-ble snake, with flam-ing eyes, That wig-gles and wrig-gles a-long the ties, The

sings a noi-sy clack-et-y song, A rick-et-y, rock-et-y, rack-et-y song, "You're
cin-ders fall in fi-er-y rain, A tun-nel is wait-ing to swal-low the train, Good-

on the track, get out of the way, go 'long!"
bye, good-bye! To-mor-row he'll come a-gain!

The Corner Grocery Store

3. There was corn, corn, blowin' on a horn,
   In the store, in the store.
   There was corn, corn, blowin' on a horn,
   In the corner grocery store.
   (to Verse 4)

4. There were beans, beans, tryin' on some jeans,
   In the store, in the store.
   There were beans, beans, tryin' on some jeans,
   In the corner grocery store.
   (to Chorus)

5. There was more, more, just inside the door,
   In the store, in the store.
   There were more, more, just inside the door,
   In the corner grocery store.
   (to Fine, end without Chorus)

Down by the Bay

Traditional
Arranged by John Sauls, Jr.

1. Down by the bay, where the wa-ter-mel-ons grow, Back to my home, I dare not go, For if we do, my moth-er will say . . . Did you

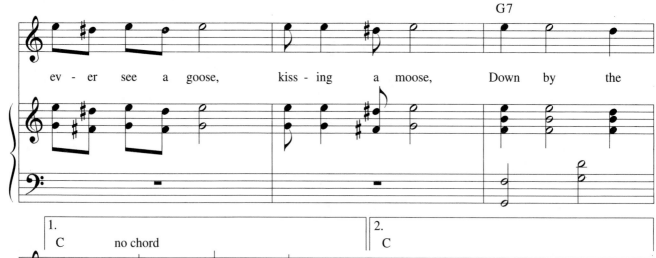

ev - er see a goose, kiss - ing a moose, Down by the

bay? Down by the bay?

2. Down by the bay, where the wa-ter-mel-ons grow,
   Back to my home, I dare not go,
   For if I do, my moth-er will say . . .
   Did you ev-er see a whale, with a pol-ka dot tail,
   Down by the bay?

3. Down by the bay, where the wa-ter-mel-ons grow,
   Back to my home, I dare not go,
   For if I do, my moth-er will say . . .
   Did you ev-er see a fly, wear-ing a tie,
   Down by the bay?

4. Down by the bay, where the wa-ter-mel-ons grow,
   Back to my home, I dare not go,
   For if I do, my moth-er will say . . .
   Did you ev-er see a bear, comb-ing his hair,
   Down by the bay?

5. Down by the bay, where the wa-ter-mel-ons grow,
   Back to my home, I dare not go,
   For if I do, my moth-er will say . . .
   Did you ev-er see llamas, eat-ing their pa-jam-as,
   Down by the bay?

Fingers, Nose, and Toes

Lightly

Traditional Words and Tune

1. Put your fin-gers on your nose, then your toes,_____ Put your
fin-gers on your nose, then your toes,_____
Put your fin-gers on your nose, Put your fin-gers on your nose,
Put your fin-gers on your nose and then your toes._____

2. Put your fingers on your nose, then your cheeks,
   Put your fingers on your nose, then your cheeks,
   Put your fingers on your cheeks and then leave
     them there for weeks,
   Put your fingers on your nose and then your
     cheeks.

3. Put your fingers on your nose, then your hair,
   Put your fingers on your nose, then your hair,
   Put your fingers on your hair and then wave
     them in the air,
   Put your fingers on your nose and then your
     hair.

Fooba-Wooba John

Traditional Words and Tune

1. Saw a flea kick a tree, Foo-ba-woo-ba, foo-ba-woo-ba,
2. Saw a frog chase a dog, Foo-ba-woo-ba, foo-ba-woo-ba,

Saw a flea kick a tree, Foo-ba-woo-ba John;
Saw a frog chase a dog, Foo-ba-woo-ba John;

Saw a flea kick a tree In the mid-dle of the sea.
Saw a frog chase a dog Sit-ting on a hol-low log.

Oo-pples and Boo-noo-noos: Songs and Activities for Phonemic Awareness, Second Edition

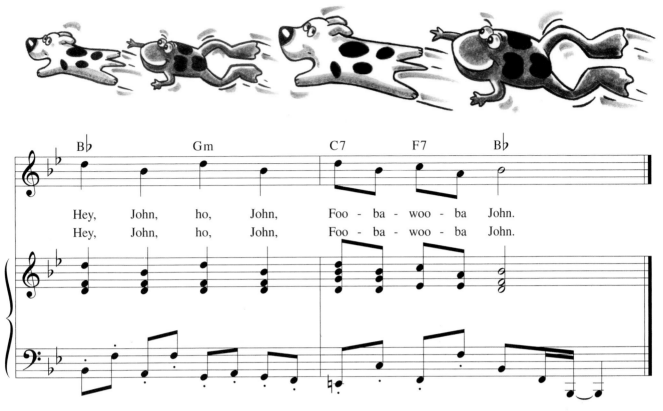

Hey, John, ho, John, Foo - ba - woo - ba John.
Hey, John, ho, John, Foo - ba - woo - ba John.

3. Saw a snail chase a whale, Fooba-wooba, fooba-wooba,
   Saw a snail chase a whale, Fooba-wooba John;
   Saw a snail chase a whale
   All around the water pail.
   Hey, John, ho, John,
   Fooba-wooba John.

4. Heard a cow say me-ow, Fooba-wooba, fooba-wooba,
   Heard a cow say me-ow, Fooba-wooba John;
   Heard a cow say me-ow,
   Then I heard it say bow-wow.
   Hey, John, ho, John,
   Fooba-wooba John.

5. Saw a crow flying low, Fooba-wooba, fooba-wooba,
   Saw a crow flying low, Fooba-wooba John;
   Saw a crow flying low
   Sev'ral miles beneath the snow.
   Hey, John, ho, John,
   Fooba-wooba John.

6. Saw a bug give a shrug, Fooba-wooba, fooba-wooba,
   Saw a bug give a shrug, Fooba-wooba John;
   Saw a bug give a shrug
   In the middle of the rug.
   Hey, John, ho, John,
   Fooba-wooba John.

The Fox

American Folk Song

go that night be - fore he reached the town - o.
grease my chin be - fore I leave this town - o.

3. So he grabbed a gray goose by the neck
   And threw a duck across his back.
   He didn't mind their quack quack quack
   And their legs all dangling down'o; etc.

4. (Then old) Mother Flipper-Flopper jumped out of bed,
   And out of the window she stuck her head.
   Said "Get up, John, the gray goose is gone,
   And the fox is in the town-o, town-o"; etc.

5. So John, he ran to the top of the hill,
   And he blew his horn both loud and shrill.
   The fox he said, "I better flee with my kill,
   Or they'll soon be on my trail-o, trail-o, trail-o"; etc.

6. He ran till he came to his cozy den
   And there were his little ones, eight, nine and ten.
   They said, "Daddy, you better go back again,
   'Cause it must be a mighty fine town-o, town-o, town-o"; etc.

7. So the fox and his wife without any strife,
   They cut up the goose with a fork and a knife.
   They never had such a supper in their lives,
   And the little ones chewed on the bones-o, bones-o, bones-o; etc.

Frog Went a-Courtin'

Playfully   **F**   **C7**   **F**   **C7**   **F** *Traditional*

1. A—— frog went a-court-ing, he did ride. H'm, h'm, H'm, h'm.
2. He—— rode up—— to Miss Mous-ie's den. H'm, h'm, H'm, h'm.
3. "Yes,—— Sir Frog,—— I sit and spin." H'm, h'm, H'm, h'm.

Bb   **F**

A—— frog went a-court —— ing, he did ride, With a
He—— rode up—— to Miss Mous —— ie's den, Said
"Yes,—— Sir Frog,—————— I sit and spin; Pray

Dm   **C**   **F**   **C**   **F**

sword and a pis - tol by his side. H'm, h'm, H'm, h'm.
"Miss Mousie, won't you let me in?" H'm, h'm. H'm, h'm.
Mis - ter Froggie won't you walk in?" H'm, h'm, H'm, h'm.

4. The frog said, "My dear, I've come to see."
   H'm, h'm, h'm, h'm.
   The frog said, "My dear, I've come to see
   If you, Miss Mousie, will marry me."
   H'm, h'm, h'm, h'm.

5. "I don't know what to say to that."
   H'm, h'm, h'm, h'm.
   "I don't know what to say to that
   Till I speak with my Uncle Rat."
   H'm, h'm, H'm, h'm.

6. When Uncle Rat came riding home.
   H'm, h'm, h'm, h'm.
   When Uncle Rat came riding home,
   Said he, "Who's been here since I've been
       gone?"
   H'm, h'm, h'm, h'm.

7. "A fine young froggie has been here."
   H'm, h'm, h'm, h'm.
   "A fine young froggie has been here;
   He means to marry me it's clear."
   H'm, h'm, h'm, h'm.

8. So Uncle Rat, he rode to town.
   H'm, h'm, h'm, h'm.
   So Uncle Rat, he rode to town
   And bought his niece a wedding gown.
   H'm, h'm, h'm, h'm.

9. The frog and mouse they went to France.
   H'm, h'm, h'm, h'm.
   The frog and mouse they went to France,
   And that's the end of my romance.
   H'm, h'm, h'm, h'm.

Goin' to the Zoo

By Tom Paxton

Gaily

1. Dad-dy's tak-in' us to the zoo to-mor-row,—— zoo to-mor-row,—— zoo to-mor-row.—— Dad-dy's tak-in' us to the

2. See the el-e-phant with the long trunk swing-in',—— Great big ears and—— long trunk swing-in',—— Sniff-in' up—— peanuts with the

3. See all the monkeys scritch, scritch, scratchin',
   Jumpin' round scritch, scritch, scratchin',
   Hangin' by their long tails scritch, scritch, scratchin'.
   We can stay all day. *Refrain*

4. Big black bear all huff, a-puffin',
   Coat's too heavy, he's a-puffin',
   Don't get too near the huff, a-puffin'.
   You can't stay all day. *Refrain*

5. Seals in the pool all honk, honk, honkin',
   Catchin' fish and honk, honk, honkin',
   Little seals honk, honk, a-honkin'.
   We can stay all day. *Refrain*

6. We stayed all day, and I'm gettin' sleepy,
   Gettin' sleepy, gettin' sleepy,
   Home already, and I'm sleep, sleep, sleepy.
   We have stayed all day. *Refrain*

The Happy Wanderer

Words by Antonia Ridge
Music by Friedrich W. Moller

love   to   go   a - wan - der - ing,   A - long   the   moun - tain
love   to   wan - der   by   the   stream   That   danc - es   in   the
wave   my   hat   to   all   I   meet,   And   they   wave   back   to
o - ver - head,   the   sky - larks   wing,   They   nev - er   rest   at

Oo-pples and Boo-noo-noos: Songs and Activities for Phonemic Awareness, Second Edition

tra la la la   la   tra la la la   la

ha ha Val - de ri,———————— Val - de ra,———————— { My
                                                          "Come
                                                          From
                                                          As

knap - sack   on   my   back.———— 2. I
join   my   hap - py   song!"———— 3. I
ev' - ry   green - wood   tree.———— 4. High
o'er   the   world   we   roam.————

His Four Fur Feet

Words by Margaret Wise Brown
Music by Barbara Andress

Oo-pples and Boo-noo-noos: Songs and Activities for Phonemic Awareness, Second Edition

Howdido

Words and Music by Woody Guthrie
Arranged by John Sauls, Jr.

do   sir, doo - dle   doo - sie, how - ji - do.

2. And when you walk in my door,
   I will run across my floor,
   And I'll shake you by the hand,
   Howjido, howjido,
   Yes, I'll shake it up and down, howjido.
   (Chorus)

3. On my sidewalk, on my street,
   Any place that we do meet,
   Then I'll shake you by your hand,
   Howjido, howjido,
   Yes, I'll shake it up and down, howjido.
   (Chorus)

4. When I first jump out of bed,
   Out my window goes my head,
   And I shake it up and down,
   Howjido, howjido,
   I shake at all my windows, howjido.
   (Chorus)

5. I feel glad when you feel good,
   You brighten up my neighborhood,
   Shakin' hands with ev'rybody,
   Howjido, howjido,
   Shakin' hands with ev'rybody, howjido.
   (Chorus)

6. When I meet a dog or cat,
   I will rubby rub his back,
   Shakey, shakey, shakey paw,
   Howjido, howjido,
   Shaking hands with everybody, howdy do.
   (Chorus)

Hush, Little Baby

With charm

Traditional

G   D

1. Hush, lit-tle ba - by,   don't say a word;   Ma-ma's gon-na buy   you a
3. If   that__ dia-mond   ring gets__ broke,   Ma-ma's gon-na buy   you a

G   D

mock - ing - bird.   2. If   that   mock - ing   bird don't sing,
bil - ly   goat.

G

Ma - ma's   gon - na   buy   you   a   dia - mond   ring.

4. If that billy goat don't pull,
   Mama's gonna buy you a cart and bull.

5. If that cart and bull turn over,
   Mama's gonna buy you a dog named Rover.

6. If that dog named Rover don't bark,
   Mama's gonna buy you a horse and cart.

7. If that horse and cart fall down,
   You'll be the sweetest little baby in town.

I Make Myself Welcome

1. I'll— tune up my fid-dle, hi-did-dle-dee-dee; I'll— tune up my
2. I'll— play on my tam-bou-rine, jing-a-jing-jing; I'll— play on my

fid-dle, hi-did-dle-dee-dee! Oh,— I can make mu-sic, I
tam-bou-rine, jing-a-jing-jing! Oh,— I can make mu-sic, I

play high and low, And I make my-self wel-come wher-ev-er I go.
play high and low, And I make my-self wel-come wher-ev-er I go.

3. I'll ___ play on my drum, bum-bum-bum, bum-bum-bum;
   I'll ___ play on my drum, bum-bum-bum, bum-bum-bum!
   Oh, ___ I can make mu-sic, I play high and low,
   And I make my-self wel-come wher-ev-er I go.

4. I'll ___ play on my tri-an-gle, ting-a-ling-ling;
   I'll ___ play on my tri-an-gle, ting-a-ling-ling!
   Oh, ___ I can make mu-sic, I play high and low,
   And I make my-self wel-come wher-ev-er I go.

5. I'll ___ play on my sticks, click-a-click, click-a-click;
   I'll ___ play on my sticks, click-a-click, click-a-click!
   Oh, I can make mu-sic, I play high and low,
   And I make my-self wel-come wher-ev-er I go.

6. We'll ___ play on our in-stru-ments, go high and low;
   We'll ___ play on our in-stru-ments, hi-did-dly doh!
   We'll ___ make our-selves wel-come wher-ev-er we go.
   We'll ___ make our-selves wel-come, hi-did-dle-dee doh!

I've Been Working on the Railroad

Very steady, like a march

American Work Song

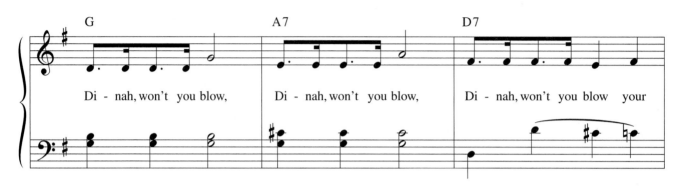

Di - nah, won't you blow,   Di - nah, won't you blow,   Di - nah, won't you blow your

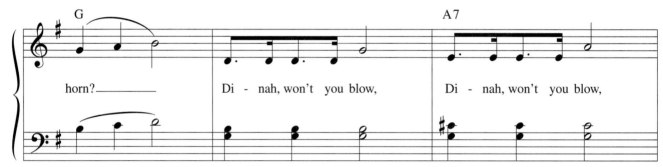

horn?_____   Di - nah, won't you blow,   Di - nah, won't you blow,

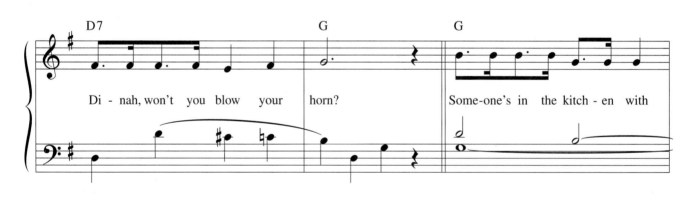

Di - nah, won't you blow your   horn?   Some-one's in the kitch - en with

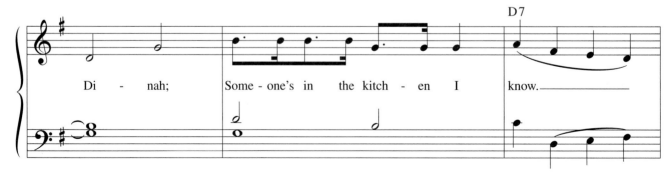

Di - nah;   Some-one's in the kitch - en I   know._____

Jennie Jenkins

Early American Song

1. Will you wear white, O my dear, O my dear? Oh, will you wear white,— Jen-nie Jen - kins? I won't wear white, for the col - or's too bright,

Oo-pples and Boo-noo-noos: Songs and Activities for Phonemic Awareness, Second Edition

I'll buy me a fol - de - rol - dy, til - de tol - dy, seek - a - dou - ble

roll,_____ Jen - nie Jen - kins, roll._____

2. Will you wear red, O my dear, O my dear?
Oh, will you wear red, Jennie Jenkins?
I won't wear red, it's the color of my head,
Refrain

3. Will you wear purple, O my dear, O my dear?
Oh, will you wear purple, Jennie Jenkins?
I won't wear purple, it's the color of a turtle,
Refrain

4. Will you wear green, O my dear, O my dear?
Oh, will you wear green, Jennie Jenkins?
I won't wear green, it's a shame to be seen,
Refrain

5. Will you wear blue, O my dear, O my dear?
Oh, will you wear blue, Jennie Jenkins?
I won't wear blue, for it isn't very true,
Refrain

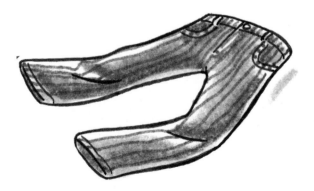

Jim Along, Josie

Oo-pples and Boo-noo-noos: Songs and Activities for Phonemic Awareness, Second Edition

C   F   C

Face   to   the   cen - ter.   Hands   on   your   knees.

F   C   G   C

D.C. al Fine

Clap   three   times   and   turn   a - round,   please!

2. Jump, Jim along, Jim along, Josie.
   Jump, Jim along, Jim along, Joe!
   Jump, Jim along, Jim along, Josie.
   Jump, Jim along, Jim along, Joe!
   (chorus)

3. Jog, Jim along, Jim along, Josie.
   Jog, Jim along, Jim along, Joe!
   Jog, Jim along, Jim along, Josie.
   Jog, Jim along, Jim along, Joe!
   (chorus)

4. March, Jim along, Jim along, Josie.
   March, Jim along, Jim along, Joe!
   March, Jim along, Jim along, Josie.
   March, Jim along, Jim along, Joe!
   (chorus)

5. Tiptoe along, Jim along, Josie.
   Tiptoe along, Jim along, Joe!
   Tiptoe along, Jim along, Josie.
   Tiptoe along, Jim along, Joe!
   (chorus)

6. Move how you wish, Jim along, Josie.
   Move how you wish, Jim along, Joe!
   Move how you wish, Jim along, Josie.
   Move how you wish, Jim along, Joe!
   (chorus)

Kicklety Kacklety

Playfully

Words and Music by Daniel Hooley

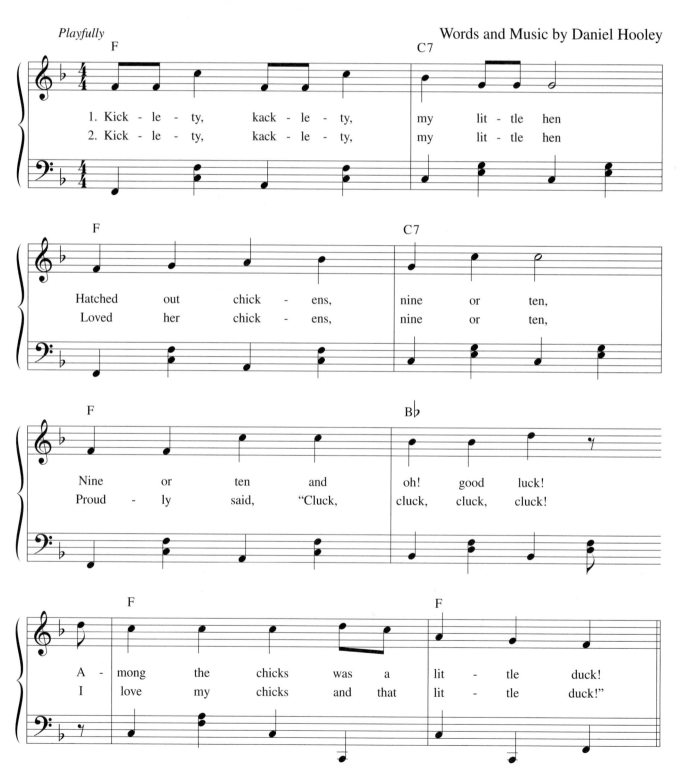

1. Kick - le - ty, kack - le - ty, my lit - tle hen
2. Kick - le - ty, kack - le - ty, my lit - tle hen

Hatched out chick - ens, nine or ten,
Loved her chick - ens, nine or ten,

Nine or ten and oh! good luck!
Proud - ly said, "Cluck, cluck, cluck, cluck!

A - mong the chicks was a lit - tle duck!
I love my chicks and that lit - tle duck!"

Refrain

F
Sing - ing kick - le, kack - le, kick - le, kack - le, **C7** quack, quack, quack!

F
Sing - ing kick - le, kack - le, kick - le, kack - le, **C7** quack, quack, quack!

F
Nine mer - ry chicks and **Bb** one lit - tle duck,

F
Kick - le, kack - le, kick - le, kack - le, **F** quack, quack, quack!

Kitty Alone

Softly flowing

1. Saw a crow a-fly-ing low, Kit-ty a-lone, kit-ty a-lone;
2. In_____ came a lit-tle bat, Kit-ty a-lone, kit-ty a-lone;

Saw a crow a-fly-ing low, Kit-ty a-lone, a-lye;
In_____ came a lit-tle bat, Kit-ty a-lone, a-lye;

Saw a crow a-fly-ing low And a cat a-spin-ning tow,
In___ came a lit-tle bat With some but-ter and some fat,

Kit-ty a-lone, a-lye; Rock-um-a-rye-ree
Kit-ty a-lone, a-lye; Rock-um-a-rye-ree.

3. Next came in was a honeybee, kitty alone, kitty alone;
Next came in was a honeybee, kitty alone, a-lye;
Next came in was a honeybee with a fiddle across his knee,
Kitty alone, a-lye; rock-um-a-rye-ree.

4. Next came in was little Pete, kitty alone, kitty alone;
Next came in was little Pete, kitty alone, a-lye;
Next came in was little Pete fixing around to go to sleep,
Kitty alone, a-lye; rock-um-a-rye-ree.

5. Bee-o, bye-o, baby-o, kitty alone, kitty alone;
Bee-o, bye-o, baby-o, kitty alone, a-lye;
Bee-o, bye-o, baby-o, bye-o, bee-o, baby-o,
Kitty alone, a-lye; rock-um-a-rye-ree.

Little Sacka Sugar

Words and Music by Woody Guthrie
Arranged by John Sauls, Jr.

Jig-gle, Jig-gle, Jig-gle, lit-tle tic-kle, tic-kle, tic-kle, tic-kle
(Jig-gle, pick-le, pick-le, pick-le, pick-le,)

Lit-tle sack of sug-ar I could eat you up.

Verse:

1. Hey, hey, hey, my lit-tle sack of su-gar,
Hee, hee, hee, my pret-ty lit-tle an-gel,

Ho, ho, ho, my lit - tle sack of sweet.
Pret - ty, pret - ty, pret - ty, I could eat your feet.

2. Hey, hey, hey, my little honey bunny,
   Ho, ho, ho, my little turtle dove.
   Hee, hee, hee, my little sack of 'taters,
   So pretty, pretty, pretty, I could eat your toes. *(Chorus)*

3. Hey, hey, hey, my tootsie wootsie,
   Wrangle, tangle, dangle and my honey in a tree.
   Ho, ho, ho, my butterfly fritter,
   So pretty, pretty, pretty I could eat your nose. *(Chorus)*

4. Google, google, google, a coo and a cuddle,
   I kick your foot, like a bicycle pedal;
   Pretty little hoot owl and a one-eyed frog,
   So pretty, pretty, pretty, I could gobble you whole.
   (Chorus)

   Final chorus: repeat "Little sack of sugar
   I could eat you up."

Michael Finnegan

Traditional

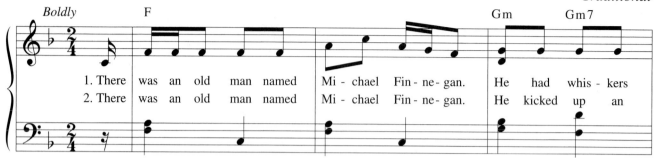

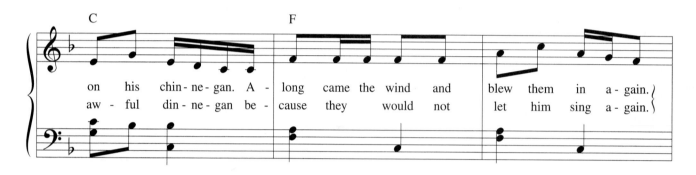

1. There was an old man named Mi-chael Fin-ne-gan. He had whis-kers on his chin-ne-gan. A-long came the wind and blew them in a-gain.

2. There was an old man named Mi-chael Fin-ne-gan. He kicked up an aw-ful din-ne-gan be-cause they would not let him sing a-gain.

Poor old Mi-chael Fin-ne-gan! Be-gin a-gain.

3. There was an old man named Mi-chael Fin-ne-gan,
   He went fishin' with a pin-ne-gan,
   Caught a fish, but dropped it in a-gain,
   Poor old Mi-chael Fin-ne-gan! Begin a-gain.

4. There was an old man named Mi-chael Fin-ne-gan,
   Climbed a tree and barked his shin-ne-gan,
   Took off sev'ral yards of skin-ne-gan,
   Poor old Mi-chael Fin-ne-gan! Begin a-gain.

5. There was an old man named Mi-chael Fin-ne-gan,
   He grew fat and then grew thin-ne-gan,
   When he did he had to begin-ne-gan,
   Poor old Mi-chael Fin-ne-gan! The end-a-gain!

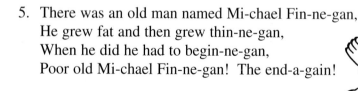

The Name Game

Words and Music by LINCOLN CHASE and
SHIRLEY ELLISTON

With a Bright Beat

The name _____ game. _____

Shir-ley!
Lin-coln!

Shir-ley, Shir-ley, bo-ber-ley, bo-na-na fan-na, fo-fer-ley, fee fi mo-mer-ley,
Lin-coln, Lin-coln, bo-bin-coln, bo-na-na fan-na, fo-fin-coln, fee fi mo-min-coln,

Shir-ley!
Lin-coln!

Come on ev-'ry-bod-y, _____ I say now

The name ——— game. ———

The Old Gray Horse

Nursery Song

1. Fed my horse in an old wood trough,
2. Fed my horse with a sil - ver spoon,
3. Fed my horse 'til___ he got sick,
4. Doc - tor said, "He's___ al - most dead,"

Fed my horse in an old wood trough,
Fed my horse with a sil - ver spoon,
Fed my horse 'til___ he got sick,
Doc - tor said, "He's___ al - most dead,"

Fed my horse in an old wood trough, And there he caught the whoop - ing cough.
Fed my horse with a sil - ver spoon, And then he kicked it o-ver the moon.
Fed my horse 'til___ he got sick, ___ Called for the Doc - tor quick, quick, quick.
Doc - tor said, "He's___ al - most dead, ___ Put this horse to bed, bed, bed!"

Refrain

Koy ma - lin - go, kil - ko, kil - ko, Koy ma - lin - go, Kil - ko kee.

Old Molly Hare

Lightly

"Old Mol - ly Hare, What you do - ing there?"

"Run - ning through the cot - ton patch, Hard as I can tear."

"Old Mol - ly Hare, What you do - ing there?"

Pounding a Nail

With a steady beat

Words and Music by Richard C. Berg

1. Rap - a - tap - tap!
2. Rap - a - tap - tap!

Bing! Bang! Bong!
Swish! Swish! Swish!

Rap - a - tap - tap!
Rap - a - tap - tap!

Bing! Bang! Bong! With a rap tap tap and a rap tap tap, With a
Swish! Swish! Swish! With a rap tap tap and a swish swish swish Back and

bing and a bang and a bong! I'm pound - ing a nail in a
forth I am saw - ing a board; I'm saw - ing a board that is

great big board And sing - ing a hap - py song.
big and strong And sing - ing a hap - py song.

Raindrops

Words and Music by Daniel Hooley

Drip - py, drop - py, slip - py, slop - py, driz - zle, driz - zle! Rain - y day!

Ev - 'ry - thing out - side is sop - py! Driz - zly, rain - y day!

Plip! Plop! Rain - drop! Such a rain - y day!

If this rain should ev - er stop, we could go out to play.

Oo-pples and Boo-noo-noos: Songs and Activities for Phonemic Awareness, Second Edition

She'll Be Comin' 'Round the Mountain

New Words and Music Adaptation by Paul and Dan Fox

With spirit

1. She'll be

com - in' 'round the moun - tain when she comes;————— She'll be
(2) rid - in' on a cam - el when she comes;————— She'll be
(3) tug - gin' on two tur - tles when she comes;————— She'll be
(4) carv - in' three thick this - tles when she comes;————— She'll be

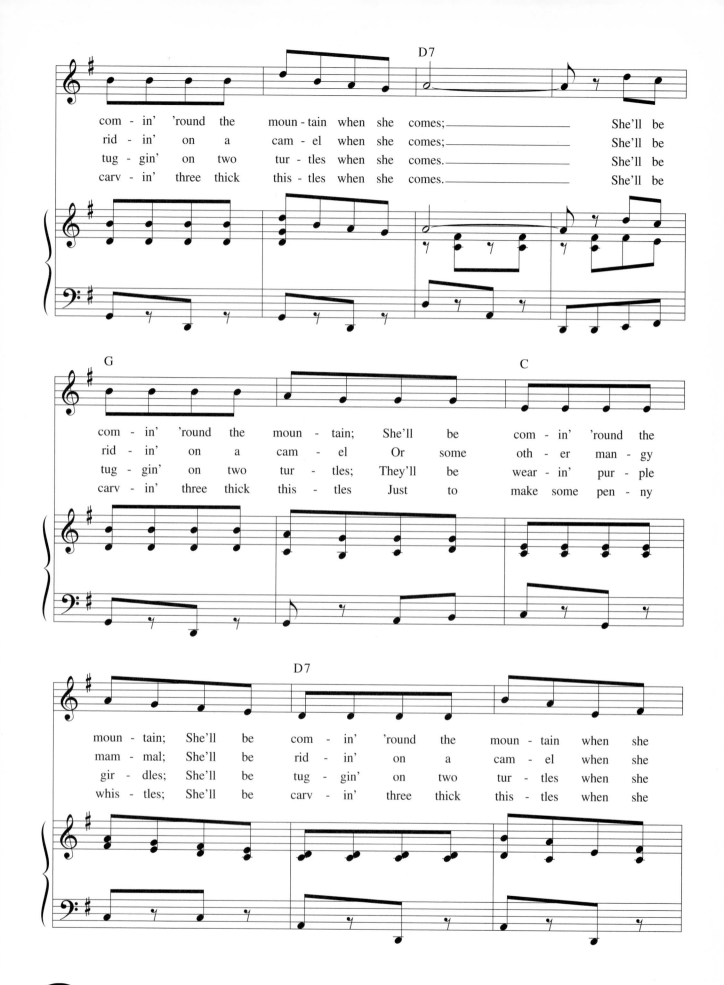

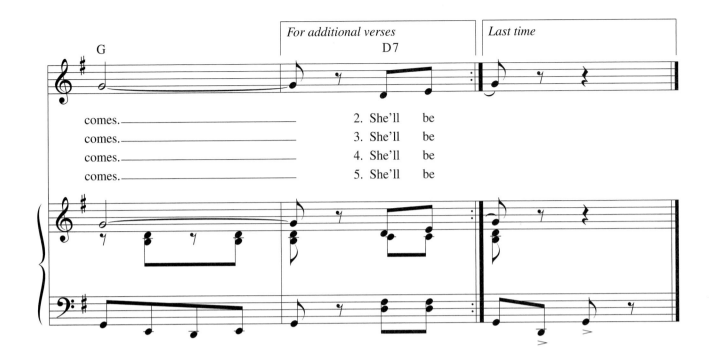

For additional verses

G   *For additional verses*   *Last time*

D7

comes. —————————————   2. She'll   be
comes. —————————————   3. She'll   be
comes. —————————————   4. She'll   be
comes. —————————————   5. She'll   be

5. She'll be feedin' five fast foxes when she comes;
    She'll be feedin' five fast foxes when she comes.
    She'll be feedin' five fast foxes,
    Eatin' fast food in five boxes;
    She'll be feedin' five fast foxes when she comes.

Additional verses are on p. 127.

This Old Man

English Folk Song
Piano Accompaniment by Kryste Andrews

1. This old man, he played one,
He played knick-knack on my drum,

2. This old man, he played two,
He played knick-knack on my shoe,

With a knick-knack pad-dy whack, give a dog a bone, This old man came rol-ling home.

3. This old man, he played three;
He played knick-knack on my knee.
Chorus

4. This old man, he played four;
He played knick-knack on my door.
Chorus

5. This old man, he played five;
He played knick-knack on my hive.
Chorus

6. This old man, he played six;
He played knick-knack on my sticks.
Chorus

7. This old man, he played seven;
He played knick-knack up in heaven.
Chorus

8. This old man, he played eight;
He played knick-knack on my gate.
Chorus

9. This old man, he played nine;
He played knick-knack on my spine.
Chorus

10. This old man, he played ten;
He played knick-knack once again.
Chorus

Oo-pples and Boo-noo-noos: Songs and Activities for Phonemic Awareness, Second Edition

TOO-RA-RAY

Traditional Words
African American Folk Song

Brightly

Moth-er, won't you teach me? Too-dum a lid-dle dum, Too-dum a lid-dle dum, Too-dum a-long!

Moth-er, won't you teach me? Too-dum a lid-dle dum, Long sum-mer day!

Chorus (dance)

Kick up and shine, Too - ra - ray! Kick up and shine, Too - ra - ray!

Kick up and shine, Too - ra - ray! Long sum-mer day!

2. Children, will you skip around . . . *etc.*

3. Children, will you jump around . . . *etc.*
   (hop, walk, bounce)

Whosery Here?

Words and Music by Kassel-Stitzel

1. Who's been here since I've been gone? Pret - ty lit - tle girl with a
2. Who's been here since I've been gone? Good— look - ing boy with a

red dress on. Whos - er - y here and been - er - y gone?
plaid shirt on. Whos - er - y here and been - er - y gone?

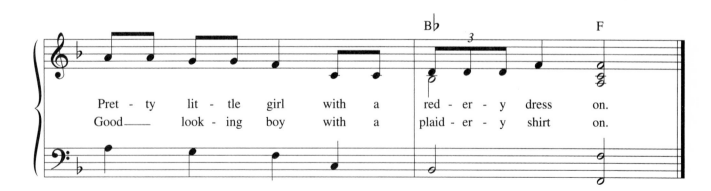

Pret - ty lit - tle girl with a red - er - y dress on.
Good— look - ing boy with a plaid - er - y shirt on.

WILLOUGHBY, WALLABY, WOO

Larry Miyata/Dennis Lee

Moderately

1. Wil-lough-by, wal-la-by wee, An el-e-phant sat on me! Wil-lough-by, wal-la-by

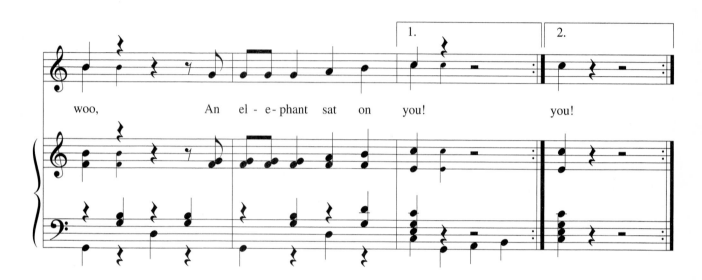

woo,   An el - e- phant sat on you!   you!

2. Willoughby, wallaby wustin,
An elephant sat on Justin!
Willoughby, wallaby wody,
An elephant sat on Cody!

3. Willoughby, wallaby, wanny.
An elephant sat on Nanny!
Willoughby, wallaby wen,
An elephant sat on Ken!

Oo-pples and Boo-noo-noos: Songs and Activities for Phonemic Awareness, Second Edition

Zany Zaddlepate

Words by Marianne St. John
Music by Anthony Burke

Lively

1. Za - ny, Za - ny Zad - dle - pate Went to bed ear - ly and
2. Za - ny, Za - ny Zad - dle - doo Did - n't do all that he

got up late, Went out fish - ing and for -
ought to do, Came to school wear - ing

got his bait, Za - ny, Za - ny Zad - dle - pate.
just one shoe, Za - ny, Za - ny Zad - dle - doo.

Bibliography and Additional Resources

Adams, M.J. (1990). *Beginning to read: Thinking and learning about print.* Cambridge, MA: MIT Press.

Bishop, A., Yopp, R.H., & Yopp, H.K. (2000). *Ready for reading: A handbook for parents of preschoolers.* Boston: Allyn and Bacon.

Blachman, B. (1997). *Foundations of reading acquisition and dyslexia: Implications for early intervention.* Mahwah, NJ: Lawrence Erlbaum.

Blachman, B. (1991). *Getting ready to read: Learning how print maps to speech.* Washington, D.C.: U.S. Department of Health and Human Services.

Blachman, B. (2000). Phonological awareness. In M.L. Kamil, P.B. Mosenthal, P.D. Pearson, & R. Barr (Eds.), *Handbook of Reading Research, Volume III* (pp. 483–502). Mahwah, NJ: Lawrence Erlbaum.

Byrne, B., & Fielding-Barnsley, R. (1995). Evaluation of a program to teach phonemic awareness to young children: A 2- and 3-year follow-up and a new preschool trial. *Journal of Educational Psychology, 87,* 488–503.

Cunningham, P., & Cunningham, J. (1992). Making words: Enhancing the invented spelling-decoding connection. *The Reading Teacher, 46,* 106–115.

Harris, M., & Hatano, G. (1999). *Learning to read and write: A cross-linguistic perspective.* Cambridge, UK: Cambridge University Press.

Hatcher, P.J., Hulme, C., & Ellis, A.W. (1994). Ameliorating early reading failure by integrating the teaching of reading and phonological skills: The phonological linkage hypothesis. *Child Development, 65,* 41–57.

Maclean, M., Bryant, P, & Bradley, L. (1987). Rhymes, nursery rhymes, and reading in early childhood. *Merrill-Palmer Quarterly, 33,* 255–281.

Metsala, J.L., & Ehri, L.C. (1998). *Word recognition in beginning literacy.* Mahwah, NJ: Lawrence Erlbaum.

Simmons, D.C., & Kameenui, E.J. (1998). *What research tells us about children with diverse learning needs.* Mahwah, NJ: Lawrence Erlbaum.

Smith, S.B., Simmons, D.C., & Kameenui, E.J. (1998). Phonological awareness: Research bases. In D.C. Simmons & E.J. Kameenui (Eds.). *What Research Tells Us About Children With Diverse Learning Needs* (pp. 61–127). Mahwah, NJ: Lawrence Erlbaum.

Snow, C.E., Burns, M.S., & Griffin, P. (1998). *Preventing reading difficulties in young children.* Washington, DC: National Academy Press.

Stanovich, K.E. (2000). *Progress in understanding reading: Scientific foundations and new frontiers.* New York: Guilford Press.

Yopp, H.K. (1992). Developing phonemic awareness in young children. *The Reading Teacher, 45,* 696–703.

Yopp, H.K. (1995). A test for assessing phonemic awareness in young children. *The Reading Teacher, 49, 20–29.*

Yopp, H.K. (1995). Read-aloud books for developing phonemic awareness: An annotated bibliography. *The Reading Teacher, 48,* 538–542.

Yopp, H.K., & Yopp, R.H. (2000). Supporting phonemic awareness development in the classroom. *The Reading Teacher, 54,* 130–143.

She'll be Comin' 'Round the Mountain, continued from page 119.

6. She'll hold six scary spiders when she comes;
   She'll hold six scary spiders when she comes.
   First, a small one sat beside her,
   Then the others tried to bite her;
   Now she's holdin' no more spiders when she comes.

7. She'll send seven stingin' starfish when she comes;
   She'll send seven stingin' starfish when she comes.
   She'll send seven stingin' starfish;
   Did you know that starfish are fish?
   She'll send seven stingin' starfish when she comes.

8. She'll ride eight overweight elephants when she comes;
   She'll ride eight overweight elephants when she comes.
   She'll ride eight overweight elephants;
   How she got 'em is just irrelevance,
   She'll ride eight overweight elephants when she comes.

9. She'll be herdin' nine fine swine when she comes;
   She'll be herdin' nine fine swine when she comes.
   She'll be herdin' nine fine swine,
   Snout to nose in one straight line;
   She'll be herdin' nine fine swine when she comes.

10. She'll be ticklin' ten tan terriers when she comes;
    She'll be ticklin' ten tan terriers when she comes.
    She'll be ticklin' ten tan terriers;
    Come along, the more the merrier;
    She'll be ticklin' ten tan terriers when she comes.

11. Oh, we'll all go down to meet her when she comes;
    Oh, we'll all go down to meet her when she comes.
    Oh, we'll all go down to meet her;
    Oh, we'll all go down to greet her;
    Oh, we'll all go down to meet her when she comes.

For permission to reprint copyrighted material, grateful acknowledgment is made to the following sources:

American Book Company: "I Make Myself Welcome" from *Meeting Music.* Lyrics copyright © 1966 by American Book Company.

Atheneum Books for Young Readers, an imprint of Simon & Schuster Children's Publishing Division: "Is It Possicle?" from *Open the Door* by Marion Edey. Text copyright 1949 by Marion Edey.

Estate of Richard C. Berg: "Pounding a Nail," words and music by Richard C. Berg from *Music for Young Americans,* Book Two.

Isobel Best: "Lilly Lee" by Isobel Best.

Curtis Brown, Ltd.: "The Bluffalo" from *How Beastly!* by Jane Yolen. Text copyright © 1980 by Jane Yolen. Published by Boyds Mills Press, Inc.

Joanna Cole: "Hippopotamus" by Joanna Cole from *A New Treasury of Children's Poetry,* selected by Joanna Cole. Text copyright © 1984 by Joanna Cole.

Dial Books for Young Readers, an imprint of Penguin Putnam Books for Young Readers, a division of Penguin Putnam Inc.: "Whisky Frisky" by Anonymous from *A Child's Treasury of Animal Verse,* edited by Mark Daniel. Text copyright © 1989 by Breslich & Foss.

Dutton Children's Books, an imprint of Penguin Putnam Books for Young Readers, a division of Penguin Putnam Inc.: "Galoshes" from *Stories to Begin On* by Rhoda W. Bacmeister. Text copyright 1940 by E.P. Dutton; text copyright renewed © 1968 by Rhoda W. Bacmeister. "Wiggly Giggles" from *Me is How I Feel: Poems* by Stacy Jo Crossen and Natalie Anne Covell. Text copyright © 1970 by A. Harris Stone, Stacy Crossen, Natalie Covell, and Victoria deLarrea.

Sam Fox Publishing Company, Inc.: "The Happy Wanderer," lyrics by Antonia Ridge, music by Friedrich W. Moller. Copyright © 1954, 1982 by Bosworth & Co., Ltd., London.

Geordie Music Publishing Company: "Bandyrowe" (Retitled: "Kitty Alone") by Jean Ritchie from *Children's Songs and Games from the Southern Mountains.* Copyright © 1964 by Jean Ritchie Geordie Music Publishing Company.

Charles Ghigna: "Snakes" from *Animal Trunk: Silly Poems to Read Aloud* by Charles Ghigna. Text copyright © 1999 by Charles Ghigna.

Harcourt, Inc.: "Whosery Here?" Kentucky folk song collected by Barbara Andress from *The Music Book,* Teacher's Reference Book, Kindergarten. Lyrics and music copyright © 1984 by Holt, Rinehart and Winston, Inc. Music by Barbara Andress from "His Four Fur Feet" by Margaret Wise Brown in *Holt Music,* Teacher's Edition, Grade K. Music copyright © 1988 by Holt, Rinehart and Winston, Inc. "If Your Car Goes" from *Bing Bang Boing* by Douglas Florian. Copyright © 1994 by Douglas Florian. "Do-It-Yourself Poem," "Keep Your Eyes," and "Pizza Treatsa" from *Laugh-eteria* by Douglas Florian. Text copyright © 1999 by Douglas Florian. "The Tiger" from *Mammalabilia* by Douglas Florian. Text copyright © 2000 by Douglas Florian. "Clickbeetle" from *The Llama Who Had No Pajama: 100 Favorite Poems* by Mary Ann Hoberman. Text copyright © 1976 by Mary Ann Hoberman. "Fish" from *The Llama Who Had No Pajama: 100 Favorite Poems* by Mary Ann Hoberman. Text copyright © 1959 by Mary Ann and Howard Hoberman. "Moses and His Toeses" from *Moses Supposes His Toeses Are Roses and 7 Other Silly Old Rhymes,* retold by Nancy Patz. Text copyright © 1983 by Nancy Patz Blaustein. "Barnyard Song," Kentucky Mountain folk song from *Holt Music,* Teacher's Edition, Grade K. Lyrics and music copyright © 1988 by Holt, Rinehart and Winston, Inc. "Jennie Jenkins," Early American song from *The Music Book,* Teacher's Reference Book, Kindergarten. Lyrics and music copyright © 1984 by Holt, Rinehart and Winston, Inc. "Jim Along, Josie" from *Holt Music,* Teacher's Edition, Grade 2. Copyright © 1988 by Holt, Rinehart and Winston, Inc. "The Old Gray Horse" from *Holt Music,* Teacher's Edition, Grade 1. Lyrics and music copyright © 1988 by Holt, Rinehart and Winston, Inc.